BUDDHIST PSYCHOLOGY

THE FOUNDATION OF BUDDHIST THOUGHT SERIES

Buddhist Psychology

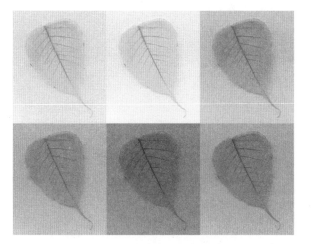

THE FOUNDATION of BUDDHIST THOUGHT

VOLUME 3

GESHE TASHI TSERING

FOREWORD BY LAMA ZOPA RINPOCHE

EDITED BY GORDON MCDOUGALL

Wisdom

Wisdom Publications
199 Elm Street
Somerville, MA 02144 USA
wisdompubs.org

Library of Congress Cataloging-in-Publication Data
Tashi Tsering, Geshe, 1958–
  Buddhist psychology / Geshe Tashi Tsering ; foreword by Lama
Zopa Rinpoche ; edited by Gordon McDougall.
    p. cm.— (Foundation of Buddhist thought ; v. 3)
  Includes bibliographical references and index.
  ISBN 0-86171-272-2 (pbk. : alk. paper)
    1. Buddhism—Psychology. 2. Knowledge, Theory of (Buddhism)
I. Thubten Zopa, Rinpoche, 1946–. II. McDougall, Gordon, 1948–. III. Title.
BQ4570.P76T37 2006
294.3'422—dc22

                                        2006020357

ISBN 978-0-86171-272-4   EBOOK ISBN 978-0-86171-961-7

21 20 19 18
7 6 5 4

Cover and interior design by Gopa&Ted2, Inc. Set in Goudy 10.5/16 pt.
Author photo by Robin Bath.

Wisdom Publications' books are printed on acid-free paper and meet the guidelines for
permanence and durability set by the Committee on Production Guidelines for Book
Longevity of the Council on Library Resources.

Printed in the United States of America.

MIX
Paper from
responsible sources
FSC® C011935

Please visit fscus.org.

Contents

FOREWORD

THE BUDDHA'S MESSAGE is universal. We all search for happiness but somehow fail to find it because we are looking for it in the wrong way. Only when we start cherishing others will true happiness grow within us. And so the Buddha's essential teaching is one of compassion and ethics, combined with the wisdom that understands the nature of reality. The teachings of the Buddha contain everything needed to eliminate suffering and make life truly meaningful, and as such the teachings are not only relevant to today's world, but vital.

This is the message my precious teacher, Lama Thubten Yeshe, gave to his Western students. His vision to present the Dharma in a way that is accessible and relevant to everyone continues and grows. His organization, the Foundation for the Preservation of the Mahayana Tradition (FPMT), now has centers all over the world, and Lama's work is carried on by many of his students.

The Foundation of Buddhist Thought, developed by Geshe Tashi Tsering, is one of the core courses of the FPMT's integrated education program. The essence of Tibetan Buddhist philosophy can be found within its six subjects. The Foundation of Buddhist Thought serves as a wonderful basis for further study in Buddhism, as well as a tool to transform our everyday lives.

Geshe Tashi has been the resident teacher at Jamyang Buddhist Centre, London, since 1994. He has been very beneficial in guiding the students there and in many other centers where he teaches. Besides his profound knowledge—he is a Lharampa Geshe, the highest educational qualification within our tradition—his excellent English and his deep understanding of his Western students means that he can present the Dharma in a way that is both accessible and relevant. His wisdom, compassion, and humor are combined with a genuine gift as a teacher. You will see within the six books of the Foundation of Buddhist Thought series the same combination of profound understanding and heart advice that can guide beginner and experienced Dharma practitioner alike on the spiritual path.

Whether you read this book out of curiosity or as part of your spiritual journey, I sincerely hope that you find it beneficial and that it shows you a way to open your heart and develop your wisdom.

Lama Zopa Rinpoche
Spiritual Director
The Foundation for the Preservation of the Mahayana Tradition

Preface

NOT LONG AGO, I received the news that my kind mother had contracted terminal cancer, and this news triggered some very difficult emotions. Even with all the Buddhist teachings and practices I had at my disposal to ease the pain and confusion, it seemed initially that nothing would help. I have been a monk most of my life, and I have practiced mind training and studied Buddhist psychology since I was a teenager, yet due to this deep connection with my mother, I was unable to see beyond my basic reactive emotions. The experience really drove home to me how powerful our states of mind are and how important it is to develop a resilient and healthy mental life.

It is perhaps a truism to note that in modern society, while we are becoming more prosperous and have more technology at our fingertips, these external means to happiness are useless if our minds are in distress. Physical well-being and the well-being of society rely deeply on psychological well-being. For thirty years I have been taught this, and I have come to believe it. But personal trauma really brought home for me how our happiness in this lifetime is utterly dependent on a healthy mind. And of course, the Buddhist tradition goes beyond this one brief lifetime and addresses the countless lifetimes of our mindstreams, aiming for happiness in all future lives until we are able to attain the complete cessation of suffering and our final goal, enlightenment.

Once I adjusted to the tragic news about my mother's condition, I was able to implement the training and practices I had been taught, and I slowly found more balance and calm. Thus the second valuable lesson from this time was not only how powerful our emotional life is but also how effective mind training can be. Without a doubt, applying the Buddha's teachings can bring about a calm and stable mind and see us through potentially damaging emotions. Despite the situation, the episode provided me a practical opportunity to test the efficacy of the theories that I have been passing on to others all my adult life. Within a monastic environment such as the one in which I was trained, it is easy to study and learn and accept without fully testing the teachings. For me, teaching in the West and encountering Western students extremely interested in therapeutic psychology has also stretched my understanding, but this particular experience revealed clearly the crucial importance of mental well-being.

This book is my attempt to make the very traditional exposition of the mind and its mental states more accessible and hopefully more useful to you. I have taken what follows from the three main sources of Buddhist mindscience that are studied in the monasteries in South India. They are: the *Abhidharma* texts that deal with Buddhist psychology; the *Pramana* texts on epistemology that address the development of understanding; and the *Vajrayana*, or tantric, texts that explore the esoteric understandings of the mind.

Buddhist masters, including His Holiness the Dalai Lama, have said that without exploration of these three categories of the Buddhist literature, it is impossible to fully comprehend the Buddhist concept of mind. My main focus will be the first two of these areas of study, the Abhidharma and Pramana teachings. The Vajrayana teachings are very advanced and are largely beyond the scope of this book. Volume 6 in this series addresses the Vajrayana in greater depth. Similarly, although I will be looking at all the positive states of mind we can develop, and in particular the advantages of altruism, I will not deal in depth with the so-called method aspect of the mind, which is the subject of the fourth book in this series.

The traditional Buddhist understanding of the mind is incredibly profound. In many ways the Western mindsciences are only starting to move toward what has been standard monastery textbook material for centuries. In fact, the rigorous presentation that has been passed down to us from the great masters is such that you might find this book a little academic. Believe me when I say, however, that this is a manual for living and is meant to be used as such. If you challenge what you read at every opportunity, analyzing and investigating from the point of view of your own experience, you will find much that is relevant and practical. The Buddhist teachings are intended to bring about a state of happiness and an end to suffering. The information contained in this book *must* be relevant to your everyday life, or it is of no use at all.

We all have some concept of the emotional and psychological aspects of our minds. With this book I hope to help you investigate more deeply what your mind is and how and why it functions as it does. I hope that you will come to see the primacy of the mind and how to take your first steps on the long road to mental peace and well-being. And by that I mean more than attaining a state of mere mental balance, but the full development of qualities such as patience, tolerance, lack of attachment, and so forth. Furthermore, seeing the ever-deeper levels of subtlety of the mind, I hope to demonstrate how immense and powerful the mind is. The goal of Buddhism is the elimination of all suffering, and for this the deepest levels of mind must be addressed and understood. By seeing the complete picture, we will then be able to devise a strategy to liberate ourselves from our problems. If we understand the mind, we can change it.

I sometimes feel that the only people interested in changing our minds are the advertising agencies, and it is clear to me that their motivation is less than positive. Yet why is it that they alone seem to know the power of the mind and its points of vulnerability? I recently saw an ad for an insurance company on British television that opened with the image of a girl's face. The face began to age, from a teenager through adulthood to the face of a woman in her sixties. As I watched this, two things came to mind. The first was how cunning the advertisers are, playing on our fears and vulnerabilities—we identify with the woman physically aging on the screen, and it's impossible not to feel that old age is waiting for us as well, and so it logically follows that we must spend money insuring our interests for those years. Second, the face in the commercial stops aging at around sixty. Had they continued to age the face much more, I think it would have defeated their purpose. The insurance company does not want us to have the full realization of the devastation that we will succumb to through time. Their aim is to scare us just enough to spend money but not so much that we give up hope!

In one way, however, I found this advertisement very beneficial, for it graphically reminds us that we all move inexorably toward old age. And just as the face slowly transforms from that of a teenager to that of a retired person, we can understand that the mind is ever-changing as well. Our mind of today will produce all of our future minds, and the way they manifest depends on how we direct our thoughts now. We have the power to influence our future.

To understand the mind and this potential, we need to learn from people who themselves have deep understanding. The masters who gave commentary on the subjects in this book were highly realized and gained their insights through studying the teachings of the Buddha. Even if you don't consider yourself a Buddhist or have any interest in liberation or enlightenment, such a study of the mind as we see in this book may profoundly affect your thoughts and actions, and the way you live your life from this point forward.

Editor's Preface

THE SCIENTIFIC PERSPECTIVE permeates our thinking and defines our lives. I grew up deeply suspicious of the worship of technological progress and the "truths" expounded by scientists. When I first began delving into Buddhism, however, I realized that I nonetheless viewed everything through the lens of scientific reasoning.

The scientific emphasis on evidence and logic is part of the attraction that Tibetan Buddhism has for many Westerners. The Buddha said we should test his teachings as a goldsmith tests gold, and many of us would accept no less. One of the strengths of the Western system of education is that we are taught from a very young age to ask, "Why?" And yet, even though the logic of Buddhism attracts us, alone it would not hold us. As Geshe Tashi emphasizes in this book, Buddhism approaches reality through reason hand in hand with compassion, and the two cannot be separated. The wisdom perspective—the process of developing a sharp logical understanding of the nature of reality—must parallel the method perspective—the process of developing a good heart.

While this book focuses on logic, the intuitive, emotional perspective is not forgotten. And while this commentary is based on the various traditional texts that Geshe Tashi studied in his monastery, it is also grounded in his rare ability to adapt this ancient wisdom to the minds and needs of the twenty-first-century reader.

When I first met him in 1992, Geshe-la was staying at Nalanda Monastery in southern France, studying both the English language and the Western mind. From his very first contact with Westerners, he wanted to know us and understand us in order to see how best to bring us the very special message of the Buddhist teachings. Born in Purang, Tibet, in 1958, Geshe Tashi escaped to India with his parents one year later. He entered Sera Mey Monastic University at thirteen and spent the next sixteen years working for his Geshe degree, graduating as a Lharampa Geshe, the highest possible degree.

After a year at the Higher Tantric College (Gyuto), Geshe-la began his teaching career in Kopan Monastery in Kathmandu, the principal monastery of the Foundation for the Preservation of the Mahayana Tradition (FPMT). Geshe Tashi then moved to the Gandhi Foundation College in Nagpur, and it was at that time that the FPMT's Spiritual Director, Lama Thubten Zopa Rinpoche, asked him to teach in the West. After two years at Nalanda Monastery in France, Geshe Tashi became in 1994 the resident teacher at Jamyang Buddhist Centre in London.

Very early on in his teaching career at Jamyang he saw that the text-based, passive learning usually associated with Tibetan Buddhism often failed to engage the students in Western Dharma centers in a meaningful way. And so, incorporating Western pedagogic methods, he devised a two-year, six-module course to give his students a solid overview of Buddhism. The book you have in your hands is derived from the third course book of *The Foundation of Buddhist Thought*.

As with the other books in the series, many people have been involved with its development and I would like to thank them all. I would also like to offer my warmest thanks to Lama Zopa Rinpoche, the head of the FPMT and the inspiration for the group of study programs to which *The Foundation of Buddhist Thought* belongs.

1 Mind in Buddhism

An Inner Science

In Tibetan Buddhism, the study of the mind is classified as an *inner science*. Psychology (the study of what the mind is) and epistemology (the study of how the mind functions) are understood to be crucial aspects of the spiritual path. Medicine and logic are *outer sciences*, and although considered very important, are accorded less prominence when compared to the inner sciences.

This is because everything the Buddha taught, and hence everything within the Buddhist canon, is meant to help us relieve suffering and achieve happiness, and that only happens through the mind. Medicine can cure the body, but that in itself cannot make us happy. According to Buddhism, even physical health is linked to mental states. Thus the real threats to our well-being are attachment, anger, and ignorance—the three fundamental deluded minds that lead to all other afflictions, both mental and physical. Only with thorough understanding of the mind and its functions can we hope to transcend the disturbing thoughts and emotions that plague us.

While the ultimate goal of studying the mind is complete freedom from suffering, we can also study the mind for more immediate therapeutic reasons. Investigating the mind by analyzing our thoughts, emotions, and so on is the first step to alleviating all manner of mental illnesses. In his first teaching, the Buddha compares the stages of freeing the mind to recovery from an illness: if we don't first recognize that we are ill, we won't seek help. And if we don't know the origin of our illness, we cannot choose the most effective therapy. The Buddha uses the framework of the four noble truths to formulate this insight: the first truth, *the truth of suffering,* is the illness. The second truth, *the truth of the origin of suffering,* refers to the cause of the illness. The third truth, *the truth of cessation,* is the understanding that a complete cure is possible. And the fourth truth, *the truth of the path that leads to cessation,* is the cure. The four noble truths encompass the entire spiritual path with all its many aspects, but we can apply them equally well to the nature of the mind. To transform the mind, we must see that it can be transformed, an understanding that can arise only out of true knowledge of its nature.

In Western psychotherapy, a patient is similarly led toward insight into his or her mental state in order to affect a cure. In this, the goals of Buddhism and Western psychotherapy overlap. But while there are many similarities, not all goals are shared. Assuming a commonality where fundamental differences exist can cause confusion.

According to books I have read and my discussions with psychoanalysts, the aim of psychoanalysis is to bring the various elements of the psyche—emotions, memories, and so forth—into harmony so that the person develops a greater cohesion of his sense of self. This is the final goal. In contrast, the aspiration in Buddhism is to rise above the very concept of self or "I." Rather than harmonizing the disharmonious elements of the psyche so it becomes whole, and hence reifying the concept of the self, the goal according to the Buddhist teachings is to transcend the very concept of the self. This is clearly a big difference.

In its rejection of the notion of self, Buddhism is radical. Buddhism understands that no matter what we possess or how emotionally balanced we might be, a sense of insecurity constantly inhabits our innermost being; that until this is addressed, it is very difficult for us to feel complete; and that the cause of all this is the false sense of self. We suffer because we misunderstand our mode of existence, and on the basis of that understanding we mistakenly infer the existence of an active, real "me." This is not to say that we are just illusions or dreams, but that the central figure in the drama of our lives—the "I" we hold so dear—is a fantasy. This concept is very subtle, but if we are ever to transcend the limited and limiting worldview we hold, we must understand what actually constitutes the collection of body and mind that we call "I." This is why Buddhist psychology places a strong emphasis on analysis.

Western psychoanalysis looks for specific causes to specific mental problems, but uses, from a Buddhist point of view, an unrealistically short timescale. Certainly the Western science of mind has evolved since Freud, but the assumption remains that a great deal of what is wrong with us can be traced back to our childhoods. That is not the Buddhist way. Buddhism does not consider the root cause of our problems to be an external agent of this life, but rather an internal agent developed over many lifetimes—the habitual tendencies of our own minds. Parenting and environment, of course, play a significant role in making us the people we are today, but Buddhism looks further.

It seems to me that Western psychoanalysis is a bit like Western medicine in taking a symptom-oriented approach, addressing specific complaints. Buddhism understands the various negative states of mind to be symptoms of a deeper malaise and tries to get to the root cause of the illness. The Buddhist approach is therefore more holistic. This approach is reflected in Tibetan medicine, which not only seeks to treat causes rather than symptoms, but also sees those root causes as closely linked to actions stemming from the mistaken view of the self (as self-existent), a view that Western psychoanalysis seeks to reinforce. The latter discipline sees illness as a disharmony between the elements of the self; the former sees the entire notion of self as the illness.

While the significant parallels and fundamental differences between the Western and Buddhist approaches must be appreciated, it is important that neither totally dismiss the science of the other. I believe neuroscientists, for example, can gain a lot of knowledge from the ancient texts; they will find that the inner scientists of two thousand years ago, working only with their own subjective experiences of the mind, devised theories equal in sophistication and complexity to their own. Conversely, Buddhist practitioners can learn much from the modern science of the mind. The highly sophisticated experiments that determine the functions of the various parts of the brain are fascinating, extremely useful, and quite compatible with Buddhist ideas.

The Mind in Buddhist Texts

The historical Buddha, Shakyamuni, frequently taught about mind, and all of the later Buddhist presentations of mind are based on the Buddha's own words, the sutras. The sutras common to both the Theravada and Mahayana traditions of Buddhism, such as the *Four Noble Truths Sutra*, refer to the mind frequently, discussing its functions and teaching us how to purify our present deluded minds and transform them into wisdom, understanding, compassion, and so forth.[1] Several sutras from the Mahayana tradition, such as the *Perfection of Wisdom Sutra (Prajnaparamita Sutra)*, deal extensively with the mind and explain how our realizations can deepen so that we can understand not just conventional reality but also the ultimate reality of emptiness.

According to Tibetan Buddhism, the Vajrayana—the intricate esoteric teachings known commonly as *tantra*—was also directly taught by the Buddha. The tantras contain many teachings on the nature of the mind, including explanations of how the subtle levels of the mind can manifest in various ways, and how they can be used to understand the ultimate nature of reality.

The collected words of the Buddha are divided into the three "baskets," or *pitakas*: the *Vinaya Pitaka, Sutra Pitaka,* and *Abhidharma Pitaka*. Each basket, though related to the others, has a unique focus, and these emphases correspond to the three higher trainings of conduct, concentration, and wisdom. The Vinaya focuses on ethical conduct, especially the monastic and lay vows and the administration of monasteries. The Sutra Pitaka is the collection of the Buddha's discourses, teachings that focus primarily on developing concentration. The Abhidharma Pitaka, written down around three hundred years after the Buddha's death, is concerned largely with the development of wisdom or knowledge. The understanding of the mind falls into this last category, for how can we be ignorant of the mechanics of our mind and expect to understand the nature of reality?

The Abhidharma Pitaka includes some texts that were originally written in Pali, the language of the Theravada canon, and some that were originally written in Sanskrit, the language of the Mahayana canon. Although the seven major original Pali Abhidharma texts have survived (thanks to the great efforts of the people of the Buddhist countries of Sri Lanka, Burma, and Thailand), the original Sanskrit texts did not survive. As the root texts have been lost, Tibetan monastics traditionally study the Abhidharma through two very important commentaries: the *Treasury of Valid Knowledge* (*Abhidharmakosha*) by Vasubandhu, a great Indian master from around the fifth century C.E., and the *Compendium of Valid Knowledge* (*Abhidharmasamucchaya*) by his brother Asanga.

The Abhidharma texts of Vasubandhu and Asanga focus on the mental events that occur within specific mindsets, the external verbal and physical manifestations that result from those mental events, and the habitual thought patterns that lead either to wisdom and peace or to delusion and suffering. The analytical process of classifying mental states into wisdom minds and deluded minds sharpens our appreciation of what needs to be developed and what abandoned.

The *Abhidharmakosha* focuses almost entirely on the mind and its functions. It describes the various types of minds and explains how many can occur simultaneously. It is also an important work on analysis, reinforcing the concept that developing an analytical mind is essential to understanding the mind and to progressing on the road to wisdom. The *Abhidharmakosha* demonstrates that Buddhism is much more than just mindfulness and meditative concentration. We need to gain a true understanding of profound subjects, such as the four seals of Buddhism,[2] and to integrate them into our lives at the very deepest level, and for that we need the analytical mind. This is the method that the Abhidharma describes.

The other group of texts concerned primarily with the mind is called *Pramana*. These are mainly epistemological texts that examine the way the mind works. The two Indian masters in this field are Dignaga (fifth century) and his indirect disciple Dharmakirti (seventh century). Although epistemological presentations of the mind were studied before these scholars' time, it was Dignaga and Dharmakirti who established the tradition systematically. Thus they are considered the founders of Buddhist epistemology.

The texts they composed, such as Dignaga's *Compendium on Valid Perception (Pramanasamucchaya)* and Dharmakirti's commentary on it, *Commentary on Valid Perception (Pramanavarttika)*, as well as the commentaries on these texts by later Tibetan masters, clarify the difference between perceptual and conceptual consciousnesses and define valid and mistaken minds. They also elucidate the epistemological aspect of the mind—how knowledge develops through the process of analysis and investigation.

Beyond the Abhidharma and Pramana sources, the mind is also studied within Mahayana treatises such as the *Guide to a Bodhisattva's Way of Life* (*Bodhicharyavatara*), composed by the great Indian master Shantideva, which meticulously explains how to cultivate great compassion, recognize and counteract anger, and develop qualities such as concentration, joyous effort, and wisdom.

Furthermore, the Vajrayana texts contain detailed descriptions of the various mental events that function on both the conscious and the unconscious levels—while awake, asleep, or dreaming, and during the process of death—and of how the mind moves from one life to the next. Through systematic examination of all these teachings, we can develop a complete picture of the mind.

While these texts are powerful tools in coming to understand the mind and its functions from as many angles as possible, the final realization of the nature of the mind can only arise through our own experience. The Buddha himself advised us not simply to accept his words literally but to examine them "as a goldsmith would test the quality of the gold." Although Buddhist practitioners see the importance of the teachings of the Buddha and other great masters on such subjects, they will not accept them without undertaking their own investigation.

Reasoning and critical analysis are the means to achieve a profound understanding of the nature of the mind. Therefore, there is no contradiction in the various and sometimes differing explanations of the mind given by different masters over many centuries. Each master has taken the ideas of a previous one as a starting point and developed a deeper understanding based upon it.

Monastic Study of the Mind

Before starting on great texts such as the *Abhidharmakosha* or the *Pramanavarttika*, Tibetan students usually study a preliminary text, called an *entering* or *introductory* text, which condenses and categorizes the root text as an aid to memorization. In the case of the treatises on epistemology and psychology, the introductory text is known as *lorig*, "awareness *(lo)* and knowledge *(rig)*."

Psychology, generally speaking, is concerned with how the external environment is interpreted by the mind. As such, it is an analysis of the inner world of our experience. Without understanding our experience of the world in which we act and communicate, there is no way we can understand, for example, the first noble truth—the truth of suffering—the starting point of the spiritual journey.

Epistemology, in turn, is the study of knowledge: how we know what we know and how we can test its validity and refine our knowledge. As such, it goes beyond the mere analysis of everyday experience to a genuine understanding of wisdom.

According to Buddhism, epistemology and psychology go hand in hand. When the study of psychology is undertaken without the basis of epistemology and the methods of practice it suggests, there is a risk that it will remain a mere intellectual exercise and not bring real benefit.

The mind in Buddhism is often divided into two categories. The first is basic consciousness, or awareness, which just means our baseline capacity for subjective experience. This basic awareness is sometimes referred to as "mind." The mind, however, undergoes constantly shifting mindstates, and these mental events are further divided into main "minds" and their associated "mental factors," which we will examine in detail in chapter 2. The study of psychology in Buddhism often means the study of these minds and mental factors. Using English terms can sometimes be confusing, since the word *mind* is used .

in relation to all the various facets of conscious experience, but context usually makes clear which meaning is intended.

In the monastery, I studied mind and mental factors on three different occasions. In my third year I studied lorig as part of my first debate class. Because I was very young and unable to really understand the different minds, let alone experience them, I merely tried to memorize all the various definitions.

On the second occasion, I studied the mind and mental factors in Abhidharma studies, using Asanga's *Abhidharmasamucchaya* and Vasubandu's *Abhidharmakosha,* which go into much more detail than the introductory lorig texts. Because these two and their related commentaries offer extensive discussion of each mind and mental factor, they are traditionally taken on much later, some monasteries even leaving them to the very last years of study.

Running parallel to my study of the Abhidharma texts, I studied the mind and its functions from the epistemological point of view based on Dignaga's *Pramanasamucchaya,* Dharmakirti's *Pramanava-rttika,* and their many commentaries. These texts play a central role in the tradition of debate at the monasteries. All of the students spent two months every year on these texts from the time we started the serious study program until the completion of our geshe degrees— one month in our own monastery of Sera and the next month joining the monks of Ganden and Drepung monasteries to study and debate.

At times this education took the form of simple list learning— Tibetans *love* lists—and at others it was the keenest of analytical debating. But whatever the level or type of study, it was the study of the mind, and its goal was to eliminate our delusions and realize our potential to become buddhas.

Why Study the Mind?

According to Buddhism, we are nothing more than body and mind, and mind is the sole motivator of all our actions and the creator of all our happiness and suffering. It is therefore impossible to overemphasize the importance of mind in Buddhism. The body might be well fed, and the eyes might look upon beautiful sights, but it is the mind alone that translates this into happiness. Conversely, the body might have pain, and other people might pour abuse into our ears, but it is the mind alone that translates this into suffering.

Certainly, if we are angry we need to refrain from physically attacking or verbally abusing the person we are angry with, but such actions of body and speech are results of anger, not its causes, and so ultimately it is the angry mind we need to address.

Since you are reading this book, you must have some interest in the mind and its potential, so I'm sure you already have some idea of how important the mind is. We all know how important a good home, good food, good friends, a satisfying job, and other external factors are to our health, comfort, and general happiness. Most thoughtful people also recognize that external phenomena alone do not rule our lives. We need, however, to thoroughly investigate just how much influence the mind has. This book can give you a start. But if you are going to really transform your life from confusion and suffering to clarity and happiness, the knowledge gained through investigation must be deep, at a heart level. Knowledge must be transformed into practical experience.

Buddhism sees the mind as crucial whereas the body is relatively less important. Of course it is necessary to look after the body, and struggling to physically survive leaves no time to develop the mind; but within Buddhist literature there is the sense that if we look after the mind well, the body will be taken care of along the way. Nurturing our own minds will also affect those around us; we will benefit family, friends, colleagues, and society in general. So benefiting all sentient beings, the goal of Mahayana Buddhism, begins with taking care of our own mind, which in turn begins with understanding it.

This is precisely what His Holiness the Dalai Lama says in a very interesting dialogue with Western scientists in 1991:

> ...There are two reasons why it is important to understand the nature of mind. One is because there is an intimate connection between mind and karma. The other is that our state of mind plays a crucial role in our experience of happiness and suffering.[3]

We all want to be happy and free from suffering. That was the Buddha's starting point and most important message in the four noble truths, through which he shows clearly that the final and complete end of suffering is possible. Although each Buddhist philosophical school has developed slightly different assertions about the mind, they all present the mind as the central player in our experience of happiness and suffering. This is true here and now, in the future, and in fact through all future lives until we free ourselves from suffering completely. So it is crucial for a Buddhist practitioner to understand the mind and then put that understanding into practice at the deepest possible level.

Furthermore, our understanding of the mind must extend to the crucial relationship between the mind and the external, material world. Failure to understand this relationship is at the very center of the worldwide environmental disaster that we are so close to experiencing. The internal workings of our mind—cognitive processes, emotions, and so on—relate intimately to how we react to our external environment. If I see happiness as a big car I might deny global warming; If I see *my* happiness *now* as more important than my children's happiness in thirty years' time, I might pollute the planet as if there were no tomorrow.

Our inner and outer worlds couldn't be more intimately connected, and to create true happiness for ourselves and others we need to shift from this current obsession with the material world into a more realistic relationship with our own minds. Learning about the mind goes far beyond studying lists and levels. It is crucial to see for ourselves how the mind reacts when it encounters the shapes and colors that make up the external world, and how it affects the external world. That is where happiness lies, for ourselves and others. That in fact is what the term *spiritual* actually means. Lama Yeshe says:

> I hope that you understand what the word "spiritual" really means. It means to search for, to investigate, the true nature of the mind. There's nothing spiritual outside. My rosary isn't spiritual; my robes aren't spiritual. Spiritual means the mind, and spiritual people are those who seek its nature.[4]

The Nature of Mind

What is the cause of mind? No matter the level of subtlety of view, all Buddhist schools agree that only a previous moment of mind can cause the present moment of mind. This is fundamental. All phenomena, mental and material, come into existence due to causes and conditions, and the main substantial cause of mind is a previous moment of mind. If you have read the first book in this series, *The Four Noble Truths*, you will already be familiar with this concept.

Buddhism does not posit an ultimate creator as other religions do, but it must nevertheless give some explanation for the creation of phenomena. That explanation is the principle of causality. Both mental and physical phenomena come into existence because they have a preceding continuum that acts as the cause. *This* moment of mind is caused by the *preceding* moment of mind. It is utterly nonphysical in nature. In fact, it is mere experience.

There are, of course, other factors involved. Buddhism talks about both substantial and secondary causes, and naturally we must remember that our state of mind is not divorced from what happens in our external world. A happy state of mind might be brought about by a nice word from a friend, or a good meal, but its substantial cause *must* be a preceding moment of mind. A good meal cannot turn into a mind.

This mere experience has two aspects: it is *clear* and *knowing*. Mind itself is actually defined in the teaching texts as that which is clear and knowing. We will look at this further below.

Furthermore, mind is not static, but a continuity of momentarily moving events that contain this element of experience. As noted above, we can talk about *minds,* which are the many mental events happening every second—emotions, thoughts, and so on—and *mind,* the fundamental base upon which those events occur. Within that continuity of mind are levels of subtlety, from the conscious gross mental events that we are aware of to the subtler unconscious events that underlie them and are the puppet masters that determine our surface lives. Even deeper is the core mind that underlies the whole of our existence. This is the fundamental level of mind that goes from life to life.

Mind Is Not Body

Whether the mind is separate from or a part of the body is a debate that has continued for centuries. Common sense tells us we have a body, which is physical, and a mind, which is not. One does the actions and one does the thinking. Investigation into this dichotomy reveals that it is not so simple.

Western scientists exploring the mind have been severely hampered by the restraints of traditional scientific method, where the rules of evidence have been developed in relation to physical observations alone. Without a rigorous and consensual method for verifying the claims of consciousness research, theories about the nature of the mind over the last century have been widely divergent. These theories fall largely into two groups: those of the behaviorists and materialists, who assert there is no such thing as mind, and those who claim the mind and body are fundamentally different.

Behaviorists assert that what we see as mental processes are in fact energy transferences within the brain that are so complex they translate as rational thought, and that there is in fact no mind. Buddhism refutes this. There are many levels of understanding the mind according to Buddhist thought, but every one accepts that body is matter and mind is non-matter. This is a core tenet. There is nothing at all within matter—whether our brain, body parts, or external things—that can transmute into mind. The different levels of explanations of mind— from the practical descriptions in the sutra teachings to the most esoteric descriptions of highest yoga tantra—are all based on the assertion that mind is a different phenomenon from the material world.

According to Buddhism, the material world is composed of the four principal elements of earth, water, fire, and wind, and the four attributes that arise from these. These labels are not literal—our bodies do not consist of mud and fire!—but rather refer to the characteristics of solidity, liquidity, heat, and movement, respectively. The four attributes are the objects of four of our five sense objects: form, smell, taste, and tactile objects.

It is impossible, say the Buddhists, that these elements are the cause of mind. The main cause must be nonmaterial. This is what we need to investigate and be absolutely clear about. Mind is mere experience—it is not matter; therefore its cause must be the same. This understanding pervades all of Buddhist literature. Mind can affect matter and vice versa, but the two are mutually exclusive. For if something is devoid of color, shape, or material dimension, it cannot at the same time be material.

That does *not* mean, however, that mind and body aren't closely interconnected. The deeper we explore the nature of mind in Buddhist psychology, the more we see the interconnection of mind and body and that certain levels of mind depend heavily on both the function and existence of the physical nervous system. This interconnection is reflected at the deepest possible level, to the point where the division between mind and body can be blurred, especially in areas such as psychosomatic illness. Nonetheless it remains a fundamental belief of Buddhism that we are a combination of material form and nonmaterial mind, and that one cannot possibly replace or be transformed into the other.

Taking the example of the link between anger (mind) and ugliness (matter), it is fairly easy to see that the mental condition of anger can never transform into the physical condition of an ugly face. Anger can cause us to screw our face up and become ugly, but the mind itself can never become the face. However, the connection between mind and matter is even stronger than this. According to Buddhism, the anger we are experiencing now is the cause for us to have an ugly appearance in the future. To me that makes perfect sense. You can see it in people who have great anger; their whole physiognomy seems to have grown out of that anger. Even if it is not ugliness, according to Buddhism, the result of anger is a life in an awful environment, such as a war zone.

Many gross consciousnesses, such as our five sense consciousnesses, cannot function without our nervous system or brain. That is very clear. In order for the eye consciousness to function as something that is clear and knowing, it depends on three conditions. One of those is the eye sense organ, a subtle material form existing within the actual eye organ.[5] In the desire realm in which we live, our entire existence depends on and focuses on matter.[6]

The reason Buddhism so firmly asserts that mind is not body is because the fundamental tenets of Buddhism revolve around the law of karma, or cause and effect. At death the body disappears. If mind and body were the same, what we think of as mind would also disappear. Without a continuum of mind, result could never follow cause; the chain would be broken. This is totally incompatible with the concept of karma. Buddhism asserts countless rebirths, and between death and the next rebirth there is an existence called the intermediate state, or *bardo*. The first moment of mind of this life is the result of the last moment of mind of the intermediate-state being. That mindstream can be traced back to the first moment as an intermediate-state being and, before that, to the last moment of mind of the previous life.

The mind that continues at death is not the most superficial level of mind, with its manifest concepts and emotions, but rather the very subtle mind—the core of our being that carries all the propensities that will ripen in future lives to determine the conditions of our existence and our future happiness and suffering.

Mind Is Clear and Knowing

So what is mind? Buddhist philosophical texts define the mind as clear and knowing. The clarity aspect of the mind, according to Geshe Rabten, refers to the "non-material, space-like nature of consciousness…completely devoid of colour, shape, or material dimension."[7] Space is also clear—without obstructions and not physical—but it does not have the ability to cognize. Only mind is both clear and has the ability to reflect or know an object. Mind here is the mere event of knowing, sometimes called *rigpa* in Tibetan.[8]

Mind can also be defined as *a subjective event that arises in dependence on the object that appears to it.* To be a subject, as this definition states, an object must be present. There can be no consciousness without an object of consciousness. This brings us to another fundamental aspect of mind. Mind is the actual process of knowing the object that appears to it. Mind is therefore not a static thing but a dynamic agent, a process of its clear and knowing nature. And it is not as if we must somehow create this clear and knowing nature. It already exists, operating constantly to cognize the world around us.

His Holiness the Dalai Lama describes the intrinsic connection between the clear and knowing aspects of the mind this way:

> [T]he knowing nature, or agency…is called mind and this is non-material…. Cognitive events possess the nature of knowing because of the fundamental nature of clarity that underlies all cognitive events. This is…the mind's fundamental nature, the clear-light nature of mind.[9]

What does it mean to say that "the fundamental clarity of mind underlies all cognitive events"? It means that our experience is fundamentally free of the physical conditions that give rise to it and of the transient mental states that arise and cease within our minds. It means the key to liberation is embedded within the very fabric of our conscious life.

How can we come to recognize this facet of mind? We can only know this when our own minds are freed from interaction with ordinary objects. To cut through to the actual nature of the mind and see it for what it is, we need to free our minds from interaction with the external and internal objects—images, smells, noises, thoughts, or feelings—that usually crowd our consciousness. We can only see the screen behind the images when we turn the projector off. Once the rest are gone, the mind alone remains as the object of meditation. If we free ourselves from the limiting relationships with the external sense objects that usually occupy it, the mind naturally becomes aware of itself.

If we want to know about a book, we must take that book as our object of focus. We have to read it, touch it, look at the cover—do everything necessary to understand it. Mind is exactly the same. If we really want to know the nature of mind, we must make the mind itself the object of focus. We can do this.

A mind cannot exist independently, without an object. By its very nature, mind is the subject, the agent, the doer. Subject and object are interdependent—without one the other cannot exist. This is why if, through deep meditation, we free our minds from interaction with all external and internal objects, the subjective mind will naturally focus on itself as the object.

The meditative techniques to free our minds vary according to different schools and different levels of practice. Sensory experiences or the more insidious mental events taking place all the time—discursive thoughts, feelings, and so on—can well be objects of our meditation; these are *minds* but not the clear and luminous mind we are referring to here. The mind that is the object of meditation on the mind is the mere luminosity that is the base of all mental events. By learning to focus on the mind free of gross conceptualizations, we can touch this intrinsic freedom and thereby begin to cut the bonds of karma and afflictions.

Conclusion

The *Dhammapada* says:

> Mind is the fore-runner of (all evil) conditions. Mind is chief;
> and they are mind-made. If, with an impure mind, one speaks
> or acts, then pain follows one even as the wheel, the hoof of
> the ox.

> Mind is the fore-runner of (all good) conditions. Mind is chief;
> and they are mind-made. If, with a pure mind, one speaks or
> acts, then happiness follows one even as the shadow that never
> leaves.[10]

Nothing good or bad happens to us unless our mind labels it such.
The state of our mind alone determines happiness and unhappiness.
His Holiness the Dalai Lama says that if we can maintain a calm and
peaceful mind, our external surroundings can only cause us limited
disturbance.[11] Notice that His Holiness does not say that once we have
a calm mind, we will never be disturbed by external things. His
Holiness presents a more realistic view. I think we can see this from
observing our own life—when we feel contented and happy, annoy-
ances such as late trains or arrogant colleagues hardly affect us at all,
but at other times, when we are depressed or irritated, exactly the same
circumstances make us furious with indignation or anger.

On this topic, Lama Yeshe says that we are able to discern for ourselves how our mental state determines our world, and not the other
way around. He says:

> The human mind is like a mirror. A mirror does not discrimi-
> nate but simply reflects whatever's before it, no matter

whether it's horrible or wonderful. Similarly your mind takes on the aspect of your surroundings, and if you're not aware of what's going on, your mind can fill with garbage. Therefore, it is very important to be conscious of your surroundings and how they affect your mind.[12]

If we wander through life unconsciously, simply reacting to whatever arises in our lives, our surroundings will have an immense influence on our mental well-being. But by beginning to understand the relationship between our minds and the objects they encounter, we can begin to use our minds to influence our surroundings instead.

2 Main Minds and Mental Factors

Main Minds

IN THE LAST CHAPTER, we made a distinction between *mind* (singular)—our general mental experience—and *minds* (plural)—different aspects operating within that basis of mind. The main function of traditional Buddhist psychology is to identify these minds and to classify them so that we can effectively manage them. A mental event that seems to us to be simple is in fact quite complex. I see a flower and that seems to me to be all there is. But Buddhism asserts that there are many minds involved.

According to Abdhidharma texts, especially Asanga's *Compendium of Valid Knowledge* (*Abhidharmasamucchaya*), minds are divided into two main categories: main minds and mental factors.

Main minds are passive, whereas the mental factors associated with them are active. Main or primary minds (in Tibetan *sem* and Sanskrit *chitta*) are traditionally divided into six types and the mental factors (*semjung; chaitasika*) into fifty-one. As long as the mental factors are active—which is almost always the case—there is no way to consciously access the main minds. They are just there as background. It is mere experience, neither positive nor negative.

There are many metaphors to describe the relationship between the main mind and the mental factors. In some ways we can see the main mind as the screen in a cinema, with the mental factors the images projected upon it. We never really see the screen because we are so caught up in the stories projected onto it. The mental factors color and determine our understanding of the main mind, which is much more neutral and unadorned.

The mental factors are also compared to busy ministers, where the main mind is the king who sits by passively. Or we can consider them the hand and fingers, where the palm and so forth is the base but the fingers operate to cause the hand to function. Each of these metaphors reinforces the idea that the main mind is the neutral and passive ground within which the mental factors—rarely neutral and usually very active—operate.

Some commentators use the term *primary mind* rather than main mind. My concern is that "primary" indicates that there must be a secondary something as well—the primary aspect being the most important and the secondary aspects somehow inferior. In my view, this term carries the connotation of the mental factors being derivative or subsidiary. Again, be careful with this. Mental factors are in fact aspects of the mind and in no way subsidiary to it. They are functions that condition the basic clarity and awareness of mind. It is the colorful storyline provided to main mind by the mental factors that determines whether our mind as a whole is positive or negative.

To observe the main mind we need to turn the projector off and look closely at the screen. This is not easy. Say, for instance, that an old friend walks into my flat. Immediately I recognize that person, and that recognition is a *function* of the mind and so is a mental factor. The main mind is more basic than this. It is the mere awareness that a possible object of knowledge—a mere entity—is present. There is nothing else but this simple awareness: no labeling, no discrimination, and no emotion.

It is not the function of the main mind to be specifically concerned with any aspect of the objective field. It is unconcerned with any of the many other things that normally happen during the process of recognition—the focus, the interest, the attitude, the feelings that that awareness creates, the labeling *good* or *bad*, the past memories, the future fantasies. The main mind itself does not label or make a fuss; it is simply aware of the entity.

Maybe *basic* would be a better term for this mind, because it is neither *primary* with the mental factors being secondary or derivative, nor *main* with the mental factors subsidiary. *Basic* suggests something unsophisticated or unadorned. Thinking further, however, the main mind is not a base as such, so that name too is problematic. The main mind is more like the stew into which the vegetables and spices of the mental factors go, to use yet another metaphor. Without them the meal has no flavor and no calories. A main mind without mental factors cannot exist, nor can mental factors without a main mind.

It is incorrect to view the main mind and the mental factors as completely separate entities. Buddhist scholars list five ways in which they are concurrent in that they share a concurrent base, duration, aspect, referent, and substance.

The main mind and its associated mental factors are produced in dependence on the similar base. This base is also called the empowering condition. The *empowering condition* is that which empowers the main mind and mental factors to operate. For something like the eye consciousness (one type of main mind), both the main mind and mental factors are empowered by the eye organ itself. This is not, as the name might imply, the physical eyeball, but a very subtle form that allows the color and shape of an object to be apprehended by the eye consciousness. It is the same with the other sense consciousnesses—hearing, smell, taste, and so on. The sixth consciousness is the mental consciousness and its "organ" is consciousness, not form.

Just as the Madhyamaka texts say that the two truths—relative and ultimate truth—are one entity and different isolates because they arise, abide, and cease together, so too the main mind and mental factors arise, abide, and cease simultaneously.[13] This is what we mean when we speak of similar duration. For the eye consciousness apprehending an apple, the object—the color and shape of the apple—arises and appears to both the main mind and the associated mental factors, abides, and then ceases at the same time.

In this case, the eye consciousness and the mental factors are generated in the same aspect. If the eye consciousness is generated in the aspect of the color and shape of an apple, the mental factors are also generated in the aspect of the color and shape of the apple. They have a concurrent referent, in that both observe the same object. If I am looking at a bunch of flowers, then the referent for both the main mind and mental factors is that bunch of flowers. It is not as if the main mind observes one thing and the mental factors another.

And finally, the main mind and its associated mental factors share a concurrent substantial entity. The same conditions that produce the main mind of the eye consciousness also produce its associated mental factors.

The Six Main Minds

The presentation of the main mind and mental factors may seem to be composed of endless lists, but the lists have a value. For if your understanding of these lists helps you differentiate the types of mind that occur in your daily life, this makes all the other aspects of Buddhist practice far easier. By refining our sensitivity to the way our minds process the outside world and discerning the patterns in our perceptions and reactions, we can begin to see through them more effectively.

The first list is quite simple. According to most of the Tibetan Buddhist schools there are six possible main minds, one for each sense consciousness and the mental consciousness.

The six main minds are:

perceptual	1. visual (eye) main mind	
	2. auditory (ear) main mind	
	3. olfactory (nose) main mind	sensory main minds
	4. gustatory (tongue) main mind	
	5. tactile (body) main mind	
conceptual {	6a. perceptual mental main mind	mental main minds
	6b. conceptual mental main mind	

Each sense organ is accompanied by a corresponding main mind. By definition these are perceptual, in that they perceive the object directly. The sixth main mind is the mental main mind, which can be either a perceptual or a conceptual mind. A perceptual mind is unmediated and direct—there is nothing between the object and the mind. In contrast, a conceptual mind is mediated and indirect—a mental image arises between the object and the mind. We will look at this further in chapter 6.

The main mind that corresponds to each of the five sense consciousnesses is *always* a direct perception. The main mind of the eye consciousness perceives its object purely and simply; it does not have the capacity to conceptualize—to identify, classify, or judge in any way. If you think about this carefully, it makes sense. When we look at something, the eye consciousness registers it. This process is direct and nonconceptual. It is exactly the same with the other four sensory main minds. Each sense consciousness only has the ability to apprehend a particular aspect of the complete object. We assume when we look at a flower that we see the whole flower, but in fact the eye sense consciousness can only apprehend the color and shape of the flower, the olfactory consciousness only the smell, and so on. This is simple logic, but it is something we rarely consider. The eye consciousness merely sees colors and shapes without labels, whereas the conceptual mind labels it *blue, round, pretty*, and so forth. In summary, this is the process—the sense consciousness perceives the object directly, and the mental consciousness elaborates with labels and conceptualization.

That is not to say all sensory main minds are correct and all mental consciousnesses are wrong in some way. All six main minds can be valid or mistaken. The jaundiced eye that sees everything as yellow is a mistaken main mind, whereas mental concepts can be valid even if they are not direct perceptions.

Although it is possible to have many mental factors operating at once, two main minds, even if they are of different types, cannot operate simultaneously. This means when one main mind is focusing on an object another main mind cannot. In this situation, if there is another main mind present, the object will appear to it but will not be ascertained. This process can be exemplified by the experience of being so engrossed in reading a book that we do not notice the traffic outside at all. Actually, we feel that we can easily watch TV and listen to it at the same time, and so it may seem there are two main minds operating simultaneously, but in fact what is happening is that the mind is switching from eye main mind to ear main mind and back again so rapidly that we experience the illusion that both are operating together.

Even though the mental consciousness can also be a mind of direct perception in that it has the capacity to perceive an object directly, I think that the mental consciousnesses of people like us are always all conceptual. There is always some kind of generality involved with the mental consciousness, in that the conceptual mind selects and filters the experience, limiting it in some way. A practitioner must reach a very advanced level on the spiritual path before the object of the mental consciousness and the consciousness itself relate to one another directly.

Such direct mental perceptions are incredibly powerful minds, and the most important of these is *bodhichitta*. According to Mahayana Buddhism, bodhichitta is the culmination of the twin aspirations of wanting to free all beings from their suffering and wanting to attain enlightenment in order to bring this about. Although both of these aspirations are classified as mental factors, when they are developed to their highest potential, they become the main mind of bodhichitta that continuously and spontaneously works solely for the benefit of others. It is interesting to note that the development of a single aspiration does not constitute bodhichitta. Neither the aspiration to free ourselves from the obscurations that obstruct our enlightenment alone nor the aspiration of wishing to be enlightened for the sake of all sentient beings alone is bodhichitta. Bodhichitta is the main mind that arises from both of these aspirations.

The Sensory Main Minds

According to Buddhism the five sensory consciousnesses arise as a result of three conditions. They are the apprehending condition, the immediate condition, and the empowering condition.

The *apprehending condition* refers to the object. For example, the apprehending condition for the visual main mind perceiving a flower is the shape and color of the flower. The *immediate condition* is the preceding moment of consciousness, which in the same example is the immediate moment of consciousness before the eye consciousness apprehends that flower for the first time. The *empowering condition* is the eye organ. Thus the five sense main consciousnesses arise in the clear and knowing nature based on these three conditions.

Note that according to Buddhism the apprehending object of the eye consciousness is shape and color—not smell, taste, or tactile sensation. In other words the objects that these five sense main minds apprehend are fixed. The eye consciousness can never apprehend sound or taste, the ear consciousness can never apprehend color and shape, and so on.

These five sense consciousnesses are direct perceptions. As such, they do not interpret, label, or describe objects. Despite the fact that they do not interpret good and bad, or right and wrong, they still have a monumental influence on our daily lives. The sights, sounds, smells, tastes, and tactile sensations that bombard us continually through our sense consciousnesses compose our entire sensory world and as such are immensely important.

The fact that they are direct does not mean they are always correct. Many direct perceptions are distorted because they lack the capacity to perceive subtle changes within color and shapes. Sometimes they are distorted by internal conditions, such as the experience of people unable to hear pleasant music because of a previous moment of intense anger. The sense consciousnesses are also influenced heavily by the frequency of our interaction with an object—the more we come across an object the more "programmed" we are to apprehend it.

It is very interesting to hear modern child psychologists talk about the impact of the external environment on a child's development. Although an infant may not be old enough to interpret the sensations they experience, they are nonetheless profoundly affected by the external world. Soft surroundings, pretty colors, and pleasant sounds all create positive impressions.

Mental Factors

The Tibetan for mental factors, *semlay jungwa chö* (Skt. *chaitasika dharma*), means *phenomena arising from the mind*, suggesting that the mental factors are not primary to the mind but arise within a larger framework. A mental factor, again, is defined as the aspect of the mind that apprehends a particular quality of an object. Because it is characterized by the qualities of activity and non-neutrality, it has the ability to color the mind in dependence on the way it manifests. Hence, a feeling of desire from seeing what is conceived as a beautiful object affects the other mental factors that are present at that time, and this colors the whole mind.

Mental factors are the images upon the screen; they are the ministers that do the king's work. The film might be a tragedy or a comedy, but the screen is just the screen. The king may be benign or ineffectual, but he will almost certainly employ a variety of ministers—some energetic, some lazy, some compassionate, some quite nasty. I was just a typical teenager of fifteen when my teacher used this metaphor and the example really stuck. It showed me that even though (like the king) the main mind rules, it is the mental factors (like the ministers) that are the most powerful influence in our daily life.

Just as the subjects' opinions of their king are affected by the behavior of his ministers, when we are considering our own minds, we are almost invariably reflecting on our mental factors. We do not perceive things directly but perceive rather our thoughts about things. And these stories and perceptions, when accompanied by powerful emotions, can dramatically color our experiences. When we are angry or happy, in fact, we may feel that our mind is *fundamentally* angry or happy, mistaking a single mental factor for the whole mind. This point is important as we begin to try to manage our emotions.

There are innumerable mental factors, each with a specific function that relates to a particular quality of the object. Tibetans often compare the mental factors to couch grass—a multi-segmented plant that proliferates quickly and underground is a thick web of roots. This powerfully illustrates the thick and entangling complexity of the mental factors.

The Abhidharma enumerates fifty-one mental factors within six groups, providing a helpful entryway to understanding how each one operates in our lives. The six groups are:

1. always-present mental factors
2. object-ascertaining mental factors
3. wholesome mental factors
4. main mental afflictions
5. derivative mental afflictions
6. variable mental factors

The title of each group describes the function of each mental factor that belongs to it. So *always-present*, for example, implies that these mental factors are always present; *main mental afflictions* are those mental factors that are the root cause of all our problems; *variable mental factors* are those that can be positive or negative depending on the context, and so on.

Always-Present Mental Factors

The five mental factors present with every mind are:

1. contact
2. discernment

3. feeling
4. intention
5. attention

Whether the mind is present for a long time or the briefest moment, these five mental factors are always involved. Some scholars use the term *units* in reference to these phenomena—the main mind plus the five always-present mental factors compose a "unit" of mind. Without any one of these five mental factors, a unit of mind could not function fully.

Contact

Contact is the first occurrence in a mental process. It is the simple act of mind meeting object. When you consider this, it is logical. How can a mind know an object without contact? To phone a friend you need to pick up the phone and dial the number. This mental factor is like the phone—its only function is to contact the object. Once contact is made, the next mental factor can note the characteristics of that object.

Discernment

The mind receives raw data through contact, but it has yet to be processed. Therefore, the next mental factor is *discernment,* which functions to note the characteristics of the object, to identify it, and to serve as the basis of memory. Without discernment, it would be impossible to distinguish between objects or recognize those we have encountered before.

Good discernment increases our memory and strengthens our mindfulness. Quite often our mind is able to make contact with an object, but because of weak discernment we have difficulty in identifying it, or if we do identify it we cannot recall it later. Discernment is always present but sometimes it is very weak.

FEELING

In reality, feeling is what drives us. We work ceaselessly for shelter, food, clothes, medicine, holidays, possessions, and so on, motivated by the wish for comfort or pleasure. Our sense consciousnesses continually pursue objects that trigger pleasant feelings. This, in fact, is the reason that our world is called the *desire realm*. Desire is a great part of our psyche. Even compassion, the crucial motivational force in Buddhism, is feeling.

Once we have discerned an object, we experience one of three feelings. Our minds are drawn to the object on a scale from mild attraction to strong craving, or our minds are repelled from the object to a greater or lesser degree. Alternately, we may fall somewhere in the middle, and feel neutral toward the object. But even neutrality is a feeling. In general, feeling is the always-present mental factor that gives flavor to the object.

Although feeling is a mental event, it is very closely associated with the main minds of the senses. The main mind of the eye consciousness can see a sunset, but it is feeling that causes us to enjoy it.

On one level we all know feeling—"I'm feeling happy," "My feelings have been hurt," and so on—but, on another level, very few of us recognize the degree to which our lives are ruled by feeling. It is said that feeling is both conditioned and conditioning. It is *conditioned* in the sense that it is the result of contact with the sense objects and the experience of our programmed responses to them that have been built up over lifetimes. It is *conditioning* in the sense that it is the trigger for almost everything we do, mentally, verbally, and physically. As the cause of every other mental event that has preceded it, which in turn causes verbal and physical actions, feeling can truly be seen as the engine that drives the endless chain of cyclic existence.

Generally, feeling is almost always associated with our sensory consciousnesses. If we have a joyful feeling while remembering a past event, although that is a memory and hence a mental consciousness, that mental state has occurred because of its association with sensory consciousnesses. We remember a beautiful sunset or an angry word, a pleasant smell or a nasty insect bite—all sensory consciousnesses.

Feeling arises through four conditions: natural condition, training, mental disposition, and personality.

Natural condition simply refers to the fact that whenever the mind meets an object, there is a natural tendency to go either toward the object or away from it. Even though the reaction may be very subtle, there is always a natural degree of attraction or aversion.

Training refers to the environmental and cultural influences that affect us and how they modify our feelings. Of course, these can be negative, such as army training that teaches us to be aggressive—but when the term *training* is used in the normal Buddhist way, it seems to me to refer to a more positive aspect. If we diminish our ignorance through study and training, our feelings become more gentle.

The next condition, *mental disposition*, refers to the fact that we are born in this particular realm because of our previous karma and therefore we have the potential to feel in relation to sensory objects. Sometimes this is called the *nature of rebirth* because our place of rebirth affects the kind of feelings we experience. For example, if we were born in the formless realm, where there are no sensory objects, we would not experience any sensory feeling at all.

The last one, *personality*, makes a big difference. A person who is gentle and mindful will have different feelings than someone who is very reactive and thoughtless. In this way our personality conditions our feeling.

These four things condition feeling, but conversely feeling conditions everything we do. It is impossible for an animal, dominated by suffering and without intelligence, to understand its world and develop compassion. Even a human being, if prone to aggression, will probably find it very difficult to meditate. On the other hand, if we meditate on compassion and that feeling arises very strongly, that will certainly influence our behavior.

On a more subtle level, the way we feel about an object is affected by each of these four conditions. Say I place a banana cake in front of a group of friends. Most of them would simply see it as a delicious cake and want to have a piece, but perhaps some would feel differently. One person might feely really unhappy because he loves banana cake but has a flour allergy. Someone else, having read articles about overeating, might refuse it. That is feeling conditioned by training.

INTENTION

Intention, the next always-present mental factor, is also called *volition*. This is the element that coordinates and directs the activity of each of the other elements within the main mind in respect to the object. Once feeling is present, intention moves our mind in a certain direction.

Intention is the factor that actualizes what feeling has initiated. If the feeling generated upon contact with an object is attraction, intention moves the mind forward toward the object. For example, I smell a ripe mango in a shop I am passing, and the feeling of attraction arises. Intention is the shift in the mental process toward buying it.

Intention is related to motivation, but be careful here. In Tibetan, the term *motivation* reflects a gross level of function, while intention is more subtle. Whatever the object, intention actually moves the mind toward it. In other words, intention, or volition, is a karmic action. *Karma* is one of the most important words in Buddhism but is often misunderstood. It refers to the law of cause and effect in relation to the mind. We may perform actions with our bodies or our speech, but it is our mental acts (and our perceptions of our physical and verbal acts) that create karma. New karma is created in every moment of consciousness because intention is always present. When, with attraction or aversion to a sense object, our minds act, we create the potential for positive or negative experiences in the future.

So intention is actually responsible for all our future pleasure and pain. If feeling is the cause, intention is the resultant action in its most subtle and latent form. Intention plants the seeds that will ripen as our future happiness or unhappiness.

When our mind focuses on certain things, it needs some kind of direction to go in, something to pursue. As when we arrive at a roundabout where many different roads begin, a decision must be made about which to take. That decision is intention. But again this decision is not random; there are reasons we choose one thing and not another.

Where does intention come from? Why do we take one road instead of another? From beginningless time, through our actions we have collected karmic imprints on our mindstreams, and these dictate our intentions. Karmic imprints act like mental habit patterns, and our unique collection of karmic imprints determines how we perceive and respond to the world. It is very important to understand how, due to these karmic imprints, intention leads us in a particular direction. Take a basic example. Because we are born in this realm with these sensory consciousnesses, it is the propensity of the eye consciousness to perceive form. If there were no karmic imprints this would not happen. This is a natural process. Just as the eye consciousness looks at form, the ear consciousness listens to sound, and so on. According to Buddhism, this does not occur merely because the eye has the power to see, which is a biological function; there is actually a karmic tendency to see things.

The strongest tendency of all is that of self-preservation. Imagine standing at a crossroads faced with two choices—a safe route and a dangerous route. The vast majority of us would naturally take the safe route, the route of self-preservation. Whatever helps or harms our sense of self colors our feelings and intentions. This tendency manifests itself most strongly at the time of death, where the propensity to cling to existence activates the karmic seeds that project us into our next life.

Habit, of course, creates tendencies. This is happening all the time. That first cigarette, which might be disgusting, will lead to another, and another, and slowly the addiction sets in. But generally the process is more subtle than that. The eye sees blue. This sets up a propensity to see blue in the future. If somehow one is conditioned to associate pleasure with the color blue, one's mind will tend to be attracted to blue things. In a crowd of people wearing different colored clothes, for instance, one's eye will naturally seek out and rest upon a blue dress or sweater. Our minds contain countless karmic imprints from our habitual behaviors over countless lifetimes. Try to remember this when seeking to understand why we are drawn to certain things and repulsed by others. When our attractions and aversions seem random, it is only because the level at which karma is working is too subtle for our comprehension.

ATTENTION

The last always-present mental factor is *attention*, which focuses the mind on a specific object to the exclusion of other objects. Attention also helps to keep the object before the mind. Without it, the mind would be unable to remain on the object for even a second.

Attention is the factor that filters information. Considering the vast amounts of sensory information we receive every moment, imagine our experience if we could not focus on one thing and exclude others. Our minds may skip from object to object from one moment to the next, but within a given moment, the mind attends to a single object, and it is this always-present aspect that is pertinent here. Through meditation, of course, we can enhance this attention and learn to direct it voluntarily and sustain it indefinitely, and this becomes a powerful tool for liberation.

These five aspects of mind function together, whether we are engaged in positive, negative, or neutral actions. In themselves they are neither wholesome nor unwholesome. Whenever there is mind, these five factors are present, whether we are aware of them or not—and they are not always obvious.

If we consider it, it is fairly easy to understand why there can be no mind without them. For mind, which is subjective, to be present, there must be an object. There must also be contact between the mind and its object in some way. If there is no discernment, there is nothing about the object that the mind can apprehend, and if there is no feeling there can be no actual experience of the object. In this case, how can there be a mind that "knows" the object?

But even this understanding reflects a very basic level of operation—so to move beyond that we consider *intention*. Finally, without *attention*, even if all the other factors are present, we could not focus on the object long enough for the mental event to be meaningful.

Object-Ascertaining Mental Factors

Within the traditional sixfold division of mental factors, the second group is the object-ascertaining mental factors. They are:

1. aspiration
2. appreciation

3. recollection
4. concentration
5. intelligence

If the first group is like the engine of the mind, this group is what really shapes the mind's experience. These mental factors ascertain the object of the main mind, taking the clay of raw sense data and molding it into the finished sculpture. How close the *ascertained object* is to reality depends on how deluded, or enlightened, the ascertaining mind is.

ASPIRATION

Aspiration, like intention, moves us toward an object of attachment or away from an object of aversion. It is the mind that wishes to engage in a particular activity and takes a strong interest in the process. It might be a conscious, discursive decision, or occur at an unconscious, prelinguistic level. But aspiration differs from intention. Although they are similar, intention is much more basic and acts as one of the fundamental aspects of any mind, whereas aspiration is a result of the many processes occurring and is not always present.

Aspiration functions as the basis for enthusiasm, an important part of our Buddhist practice. For example, hearing that it is possible to end samsara, the cycle of suffering, we become inspired and aspire toward that achievement. This is indeed a powerful mind, though the end of samsara will not come about through aspiration alone, no matter how fervent. We will need to employ other means as well.

APPRECIATION

If aspiration is the wish to attain or possess the object, *appreciation* is the mental factor that develops that mind. Seeing that the ascertained object has qualities that are worthwhile (and remember this can be positive or negative), appreciation stabilizes the relationship with the object by directing the mind toward it more forcefully.

Appreciation has the function of desiring the object and securing its recollection. Say you are reading this in your living room, and on the coffee table in front of you are a great assortment of objects. What directs your eye consciousness toward one object? Recollecting that scene later, what mental factor is responsible for one object being remembered clearly but not another? Feeling is just that—attachment, aversion, or indifference to an object. Appreciation takes this one stage further in recognizing the quality in the object that has triggered that feeling, and in doing so moves the mind toward holding the object. It "appreciates" the object in the recognition of the quality, whether positive, negative, or neutral.

RECOLLECTION

Recollection is the ability of the mind to return to the object. It is different from appreciation in that appreciation can ascribe a quality to the object but does not have the ability to return to the object, either moment by moment or at a future time.

Without recollection we could never know an object for more than one moment. Recollection is the ability of the mind to return to the object again and again, which is in fact what happens continuously as we are observing an object. As we will see in chapter 7, the first moment of a mind encountering an object, according to the Pramana texts, is distinguished from the subsequent moments in that they are more powerful, the subsequent moments relying on the initial experience and so not creating the same impact on the mindstream. This is quite academic, and perhaps it is enough here to stay with the ordinary usage of the word "moment." Intuitively it seems our mind stays on an object, whereas in fact it is a continuous process of returning to the object, which is what the texts call *recollection*. Recollection is also the basis for memory. If the recollection of an experience is strong, it will be easier to repeat the experience later.

The continuous application of recollection acts as the basis for concentration, and the ability of recollection to return to the object at a later date is also the basis for memory.

For example, when you enter the gompa of a Tibetan monastery, the strong Tibetan incense has a very distinctive smell. If it is your first visit, you are not actually *recollecting* the smell; it is being stored in your memory. Whenever you smell that incense in the future you find yourself back in that gompa—it is your recollection that takes you there. If you associate the smell with peace and happiness, that feeling will arise in your mind. If you are allergic to incense, however, you may just remember sneezing!

CONCENTRATION

Although we call this mental factor *concentration*, that may be slightly misleading, as *concentration* often refers to a consciously willed activity. Concentration in this context is merely the ability of the mind to remain on the object. If recollection brings us back to the object again and again, concentration has the sense of holding that object.

Our ability to hold the object is completely dependent on our connection with the experience. For example, if we are trying to focus on the wish to be free from samsara but the motivation is not really there, our minds will move to another object quite readily. I personally have no problem moving my mind from one thing to another; staying on an object is another matter.

INTELLIGENCE

As with the word concentration, the common usage of the word intelligence differs from the meaning intended here. Conventionally, *intelligence* is the opposite of stupidity. Here we are talking about something more subtle: the ability of the mind to examine an object and determine its value, by seeing that the object has certain characteristics that make it attractive or repulsive (or neither). In determining the characteristics of the object, this mental factor has a degree of certainty. Other mindstates muster information about the object; this mindstate makes decisions based on that.

The always-present mental factors are present whether we are focused or not. The object-ascertaining mental factors, in contrast, are not. Their presence is dependent on the degree to which our minds explore the object. Not falling into the category "always-present" suggests that they do not all operate in every mental event, and traditionally this is what is stated, but I feel that generally these five factors will almost always operate. If we have any focus at all (and unless we are unconscious there is usually some focus), then all five must be operating. However, they do operate at different degrees—some very actively, some hardly at all. Perhaps, for example, our aspiration to progress on the spiritual path might be very strong, but our intelligence is low, or vice versa.

Whether we are aware of these mental factors depends on the length of time they occur in our mindstream. For example, if the first, aspiration—in this case let's say the aspiration to attain liberation—remains for a while, we might recognize that it is there.

Whereas it may look as though these five object-ascertaining mental factors are sequential—that one is built on the previous—in fact they are not. The order in which they arise depends on the circumstances.

Although the terms for the mental factors seem indicative of virtuous minds, these mental factors by themselves (like the always-present mental factors) are neither intrinsically virtuous nor intrinsically nonvirtuous. The mind that precedes the action of stealing needs some kind of aspiration, recollection, and intelligence, and the mind that precedes the action of giving requires the same.

The object-ascertaining mental factors are cognitive, psychological activities that constitute the basic mechanism of our awareness. Under normal circumstances, it is difficult for us to see this mechanism operating. We are confounded by cultural conditioning, which loads us with assumptions, and confused by language, which limits our experience of an event or object by simplistic naming and verbal describing. We often perceive a secondary mental factor as a main mind. We say "I am angry" or "I am happy" and due to language we feel that we *are* that anger. To understand that this is not so we need to move beyond the assumptions we make on the level of our basic, superficial emotions and examine the more complex levels of our minds at work.

3 MENTAL AFFLICTIONS

Variable Mental Factors

OF THE SIX CATEGORIES of mental factors (always-present, object-ascertaining, wholesome, main mental afflictions, derivative mental afflictions, and variable) we have covered the first two. Before we look in depth at the wholesome and unwholesome mental factors that dominate our lives, I would like to summarize the minds of the last category, variable mental factors, which can be wholesome, unwholesome, or neutral.

SLEEP

The first variable mental factor is *sleep*, which in Buddhism is seen as the mind that usually operates when our gross sensory consciousnesses cease their functions. Buddhism believes that consciousness continues during sleep, whether we are dreaming or not, even though we are not "conscious" of what is going on around us.

According to the Abhidharma texts, sleep is seen as virtuous, nonvirtuous, or neutral depending on the immediately preceding consciousness—the mind just prior to sleep. That mind makes a huge difference to the mind of sleep. If the mind before sleep is virtuous, such as the thought that we will sleep not just to rest but to refresh the body in order to have the energy to help ourselves and others, then our sleeping mind will more likely be virtuous. Similarly, if we fall asleep with a mind wholly bent on liberation, that is a wonderful way to ensure that our entire sleeping time is very positive, no matter how long we sleep. For those of us who love to sleep, perhaps that is the best practice!

In contrast, if the mind prior to sleep is nonvirtuous—say we fall asleep while plotting revenge for some harm—then the mind of sleep will be nonvirtuous. Likewise, if we move into the sleep state with a neutral mind, then the sleep will be neutral too.

REGRET

In Buddhism, *regret* is not guilt. Guilt is an ego-driven emotion and as such is always nonvirtuous, but regret can be either virtuous or non-virtuous. It is virtuous when we have a strong regret for the negative things we have done in the past, consciously or unconsciously, acting under the power of attachment, anger, jealousy, and the like. To see that the harmful actions of body, speech, and mind are negative and should be avoided, and to feel regret that we have done them is posi-tive in that it leaves a definite imprint on our mindstreams that will help us to avoid such actions in the future. When monks and nuns per-form the twice-monthly practice to purify their vows, regret for bro-ken vows is the main practice. In Vajrayana practice, regret is the main element in any purification practice.

In contrast, if we deeply regret a wholesome deed we have done, then that is a negative mental factor. For example, if we spontaneously benefit many people during a natural disaster, but later on, for what-ever reason, we regret doing it, then that is unwholesome regret. That mind will create a big impact on our consciousness, and should a sim-ilar incident occur, we will be reluctant to become involved.

General Examination

General examination is a mind that explores an object—the things and events that make up our daily lives—but not in a deeply analytical way. It is virtuous or nonvirtuous depending on the motivation. Perhaps we are feeling joy, and we see that the joy comes from helping a friend. There is no deep analysis of why we feel that emotion but just a sense that this is this because of that, and because the action was positive, the mind that examines it is positive. Conversely, examining a mind that is angry at helping, or joyful at stealing is considered a negative mind. Of course, the general examination that sees anger as a destructive emotion is not a negative mind.

Precise Analysis

Precise analysis is the mental factor that explores objects in a detailed way. For example, we become attached to an object such as a new car and we intently analyze ways of acquiring it, or, conversely, we see how important understanding emptiness is, and we analyze in detail the strategies needed to acquire a deep understanding of it.

The last two variable mental factors, general examination and precise analysis, are degrees of the same mind, and their polarity is determined by the object they are exploring. If the object is wholesome, the mind is wholesome and vice versa.

The Three Zones

Before we examine wholesome mindstates (the third category of mental factors) we will consider the unwholesome ones, which are divided in the Abhidharma texts into the main mental afflictions and the various derivative mental afflictions that arise from them.

Each of the mental afflictions is considered destructive or unwholesome; they are the mental states that cause our suffering. If you examine the list on pages 48–49 without deep consideration, however, you might question the inclusion of some items. Since you are reading this book, I suspect you grant that desire causes problems. But if so, you are probably in the minority in the West, at least if the media are any indication. And how many counseling gurus inform us that anger is beneficial? Certainly, suppressing anger is dangerous, but to me it seems quite shortsighted to suggest that venting anger is psychologically healthy. Releasing it may perhaps solve short-term problems and release tension—Buddhism doesn't deny that—but it definitely will not lead to the complete cessation of suffering, and it could actually intensify suffering.

The chart shows the way the recognizable feelings and emotions that are on the surface of our consciousnesses are in fact triggered by deeper and deeper mental factors, starting with the main mental afflictions. I have included many more than the traditional twenty derivative afflictions, which you will find in their usual grouping in the appendix.

In the next chapter we will examine methods to manage specific negative mindstates, especially anger, but for now it is important to begin with some clarity about their origin. Therefore, I have modified the traditional division between main and derivative afflictions into three zones of decreasing subtlety. The first zone encompasses the afflictions on the deepest level of mind. The mental afflictions of this zone are the most difficult to understand and to eliminate. They are the cause of the mental factors in the second zone, which in turn are the cause of the mental factors in the third zone, the most superficial level of mind.

In the four noble truths, the Buddha taught the truth of suffering before the truth of its cause—the origin of suffering—because we have to recognize suffering before we are compelled to seek its cause. In the same way, in our everyday lives we recognize well that we have problems and negativity, and to try to understand what causes them in order to overcome them, we must delve below the surface. We will never be completely successful in dealing with the gross afflictions of envy, pride, low self-esteem, and so forth until we can identify and control their source.

Say an overwhelming desire for vengeance is dominating your mindstream. To trace its cause, look at the third zone in the chart below—vengeance is in the box titled *derived from anger*. Although there are many aspects to the mind seeking vengeance, it is principally an angry mental state. Trace that back and see that it arises due to an ignorance of the gross level of cause and effect, which itself comes from a mental factor of the second zone, in this case agitation and aversion. Although the word *anger* might not seem as strong as *vengeance* to us, anger is the root because it is more deep-seated—it has the ability to produce a mind wishing revenge.

Both of these in turn are produced by one of the most deep-rooted mental factors of the first zone, *aversion*. We are now at the very source of all our problems, the aversion triggered by our fundamental confusion about the ways things—self, phenomena, and events—really exist.

In the chart, although the derivative afflictions are arranged in an order that reflects their dependence on the deeper afflictions they have arisen from, the distinctions between the groupings are not actually clear-cut; they are given here as a guide. The main trigger for revenge, for instance, might be envy caused by attachment. We need to keep this in mind when we examine the afflictions individually.

UNWHOLESOME MENTAL FACTORS

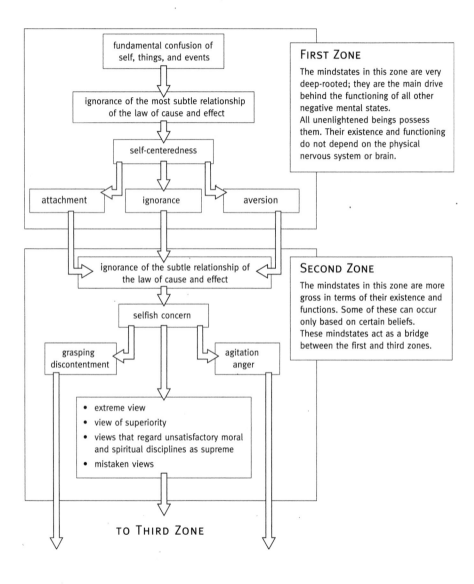

fundamental confusion of self, things, and events

FIRST ZONE

The mindstates in this zone are very deep-rooted; they are the main drive behind the functioning of all other negative mental states.
All unenlightened beings possess them. Their existence and functioning do not depend on the physical nervous system or brain.

ignorance of the most subtle relationship of the law of cause and effect

self-centeredness

attachment   **ignorance**   **aversion**

ignorance of the subtle relationship of the law of cause and effect

SECOND ZONE

The mindstates in this zone are more gross in terms of their existence and functions. Some of these can occur only based on certain beliefs. These mindstates act as a bridge between the first and third zones.

selfish concern

grasping discontentment   **agitation anger**

- extreme view
- view of superiority
- views that regard unsatisfactory moral and spiritual disciplines as supreme
- mistaken views

TO THIRD ZONE

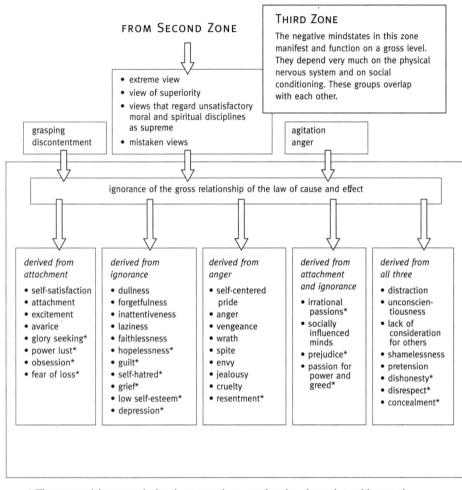

FROM SECOND ZONE

THIRD ZONE

The negative mindstates in this zone manifest and function on a gross level. They depend very much on the physical nervous system and on social conditioning. These groups overlap with each other.

- extreme view
- view of superiority
- views that regard unsatisfactory moral and spiritual disciplines as supreme
- mistaken views

grasping
discontentment

agitation
anger

ignorance of the gross relationship of the law of cause and effect

derived from attachment

- self-satisfaction
- attachment
- excitement
- avarice
- glory seeking*
- power lust*
- obsession*
- fear of loss*

derived from ignorance

- dullness
- forgetfulness
- inattentiveness
- laziness
- faithlessness
- hopelessness*
- guilt*
- self-hatred*
- grief*
- low self-esteem*
- depression*

derived from anger

- self-centered pride
- anger
- vengeance
- wrath
- spite
- envy
- jealousy
- cruelty
- resentment*

derived from attachment and ignorance

- irrational passions*
- socially influenced minds
- prejudice*
- passion for power and greed*

derived from all three

- distraction
- unconscien- tiousness
- lack of consideration for others
- shamelessness
- pretension
- dishonesty*
- disrespect*
- concealment*

* Those mental factors marked with an asterisk are not found in the traditional listing of fifty-one mental factors but have been added to show how they relate to the traditional list.

The First Zone and the Three Main Mental Afflictions

The main mental afflictions are said to be the root disturbance within the mind that leads to the manifest agitation in our consciousness. Our fundamental confusion triggers the very basic afflictions like aversion and attachment, which then lead to deep-seated emotions like anger and desire. From this root, all the other disturbing emotions arise.

If we try to deal only with our overt problems, it is very difficult to see this. But if we look deeply, we will discover the three basic causes of our present problems: ignorance, attachment, and aversion. These three main mental afflictions are also called the *three poisons*, because everything contaminated by them brings suffering in its wake. *Attachment* refers to clinging to things that support our sense of permanence. *Aversion* refers to pushing away things that harm our sense of permanence. *Ignorance* is that very sense of permanence and, although listed with the other two as an equal, can also be seen as their main cause.

Traditionally there are six main mental afflictions, the other three being self-importance, afflicted view, and afflicted indecision, but as these all stem in some way from ignorance, we can set them aside at present.[14] Ignorance, attachment, and aversion, in one way or another, nourish all the other unwholesome mental factors in our mental continuum.

If you look at the first zone in the chart, you will see that the fundamental confusion about the way self, things, and events exist creates ignorance of the most subtle relationship of the law of cause and effect. From this ignorance grows self-centeredness. We see self as permanent and concrete, and feel compelled to defend it as such. This happens in three ways. If something seems to support our sense of permanence, the mind it is attracted to it. So from *self-centeredness* in the chart, an arrow goes to *attachment*. Alternatively, the mind rejects anything that does not support its sense of permanence. This manifests as a subtle rejection of the object, which is *aversion* in the chart. If the object or event neither supports nor threatens the sense of permanence, then the mind simply ignores it.

The minds in the first zone are extremely deep-rooted, functioning well below the conscious level. All unenlightened beings experience these minds, even those in the formless realm, who lack a physical body.

IGNORANCE

In our studies of Buddhist philosophy, we hear the statement that ignorance is the root of all suffering so often that we could be tempted to accept it without really seeking out its meaning. The four noble truths explains ignorance in the presentation of the truth of the origin of suffering, and it is divided into two kinds: innate and (intellectually) acquired.

Intellectually acquired ignorance, as the name implies, is ignorance that arises from the influence of our culture, environment, religion, or training. Among the two forms of ignorance, this form is coarser and more easily overcome.

Innate ignorance is akin to the fundamental confusion at the top of the chart above. It has been part of our experience since beginningless times, prompting us to act in unskillful ways. This is the mind that innately misapprehends the self as existing independently or inherently. It is also called *the false view of the transitory collection.* In fact, we are nothing more than our five aggregates—form, feeling, discrimination, compositional factors, and consciousness—and this collection is ever-changing. Our grasping at the innate wrong view that perceives the opposite of this is the root of cyclic existence.

Seeing things as permanent and independent, we build a strong distinction between ourselves and the outside world, a distinction that does not in fact exist. This is basic ignorance, and holding this to be true, the mind defends itself by clinging to things that reinforce this position and rejecting things that harm it. It is from this perspective that ignorance is considered the cause of attachment and aversion.

Simply attaining an intellectual understanding of the term ignorance is a challenge, but setting about overcoming it in our own minds is a much larger task. Within the two aspects of the path to enlightenment, method and wisdom, practices for prevailing over ignorance are encompassed within the category of wisdom. Wisdom refers to the unmistaken understanding of how things exist, and ignorance is the primary hindrance to wisdom.

Innate ignorance arises on the basis of the mistaken notion that our "self" is a unitary "thing" that exists in an objective and independent way. This immensely powerful propensity to see things as independent and intrinsic carries on in our minds from one life to another and is the main reason that we are not enlightened.

Innate ignorance is the immediate cause of the next most subtle affliction, the ignorance of the most subtle relationship of the law of cause and effect. This is the ignorance that is referred to in the first link of the twelve links of dependent origination, the teaching that explains the succession of causes and effects that compose cyclic existence. In this teaching, ignorance creates karma, the second link, which leads to consciousness and so on through the formation of feeling and clinging to birth, which is the immediate cause of aging and death.[15] To eliminate death, we need to eliminate birth, and to do that we need to eliminate clinging and all of its preceding links. Even then, as arhats, we are still not enlightened because the first link of ignorance remains. This means that the subtle residue of the afflictions has yet to be purified.

ATTACHMENT

Attachment can arise in relation to any object and manifests in all three zones. It is a pervasive aspect of our mental experiences. Some levels of attachment are deeply unconscious and influence our actions in ways we do not comprehend; other levels are easily recognizable. Attachment exaggerates the quality of the object and moves the mind toward that object. In order for attachment to be present, the object need not be attractive intrinsically. The mind can be attracted to any object, from a gun to a Van Gogh painting.

Because of its characteristic exaggeration of the object's appeal, attachment is an agent for discontent. Before we possess the object, the mind is agitated with desire; once we have the object, the desirable qualities of the object seem to fade (although in reality they were never there in the first place), or we live with the fear of losing it. Look honestly at the possessions and relationships that define your life and explore whether this is true. Is that desire for your car as strong now as when you first bought it? Does your cassette player continue to give you satisfaction now that there are CD and MP3 players?

The same thing tends to be true for everyone. Due to our fundamental state of discontent, we grasp at a new object, anticipating that it will be the source of happiness, and we desire it. We get it, and sooner or later, because the happiness it brings is only partial and temporary, we lose interest. Then we focus on the next object down the line that seems to be the answer to our prayers. In this way, we establish a pattern in our lives of ever-increasing discontent and ever-increasing craving. The source of this cycle of discontent is the attachment that exaggerates the qualities of objects, which is in turn caused by our fundamental ignorance of the way that ourselves and the objects we interact with really exist.

AVERSION

Aversion is also an exaggeration of an object that arises from the fundamental ignorance of the way self and things exist. This time, however, because the object harms the self's notion of permanence, the mind exaggerates its negative qualities. Again, this mind of aversion can range from very gross to very subtle, spanning all three zones of negative mental factors.

Discontent becomes attachment when the object appears attractive. Aversion or anger arises when something thwarts our desire or otherwise threatens our self-image. At an unconscious level, the threat to our innate sense of self is best understood as a subtle but pervasive sense of dissatisfaction, a nagging feeling that something is not quite right. When aggravated, this underlying dissatisfaction gives rise to frustration, an increase in aversion, and overt outbursts of anger. Such outbursts invariably plant particularly heavy karmic propensities in our minds, and thus understanding how to defuse aversion before it escalates is crucial.

The Second Zone

Closer to the conscious world we inhabit but still deeply buried in our unconscious are mental factors that affect our conscious feelings and emotions more directly. These are the mindstates I have placed in the second zone, the bridge between the main causes and the surface afflictions. You will see in the chart that these mental factors are more gross in their existence and functions than corresponding ones in the first zone. It is possible for ordinary people to recognize them, but not without investigation; they are generally still too subtle and deep to be overtly noticeable.

Again, each zone relates to a different level of subtlety of the mind. In the third zone, the law of cause and effect becomes apparent based on outward appearances alone. We see somebody who is rich and living a happy life and we can trace the cause back to their good job and pleasant personality. We see this life's immediate causes and conditions but are unable to see the causes of *those* things.

The mental factors of the second zone are subtler, and so is the understanding of the law of cause and effect that corresponds to them. From the perspective of the second zone, we can see that the rich lifestyle and pleasant personality of a fortunate person has been caused by habits such as generosity in previous lives. Thorough analysis will bring us an understanding of the subtle laws of cause and effect that operate here. In contrast, the cause and effect that is perceived by the mental factors of the first zone is incredibly subtle. It is said that only buddhas can understand it at this level.

There are three groups of mental factors in the second zone: (1) selfish concern, (2) grasping and discontentment, and (3) agitation and anger. These mental factors are similar to those in the first zone but grosser. Conversely, they are much more subtle than those in the third zone.

The mindstates of the second zone occur spontaneously in our lives. We do not have to be taught to grasp at something, nor are we taught to be unhappy when things go wrong or to have self-concern and fear. Whereas the mental factors in the first zone are far too subtle for us to be aware of, we can observe the second-zone ones at work by paying careful attention to our mental processes.

Without a thorough understanding of past and future lives, it is impossible to see beyond our most superficial mental states—those of this lifetime that arise as a result of external circumstances such as our environment, friends, or culture. Investigating these alone will not help us understand the origin of mental factors whose root causes are not the events of this life but the propensities in our mindstream from countless previous lives. Because of the habits of grasping, discontent, and selfish concern, these mindstates have developed and deepened over lifetimes.

Grasping and discontent are caused by selfish concern, which in turn is a product of ignorance of the subtle relationship of the law of cause and effect. Thus, grasping and discontent are linked to the attachment in the first zone. In the same way, agitation and anger are linked to first-zone aversion.

Selfish concern can be considered from the point of view of the following divisions:

1. extreme view
2. view of superiority
3. views that regard unsatisfactory moral and spiritual disciplines as supreme
4. mistaken views

These four are wrong views that can easily arise if we are ignorant of the subtle relationship between cause and effect. They pervade our lives in many ways and color our reactions and emotions. These views are wrong precisely because they are driven by selfish concern.

The first of these views, *extreme view*, is linked with the other views in this category, but particularly with the last one, wrong view. For this, a person not only holds some kind of wrong view, but moreover holds it to be absolute in some way. The various concepts of what the "I" is reflect this. On the one hand, someone might feel the "I" to be completely separate from the mind/body aggregates, which from a Buddhist perspective is a wrong view, but superimposed on that is the sense that this independent "I" is somehow eternal and divine—that through life after life, the "I" remains unchanging. Conversely, the view of the "I" might be that it exists only for this lifetime, again a wrong view, but deemed extreme here because it is linked to a national or racial identity, in that it will cease to exist when that nation or race ceases.

This, of course, comes from attempts by early Buddhist philosophers to disprove the views of the non-Buddhist schools, but we can see the same thing happening in the modern world. National or racial identity is an important issue for many people, and it has been used to create incredibly powerful prejudice where groups of people feel themselves to be uniquely superior to others. Right-wing dictatorships work on the idea that the followers of that particular group have some divine right and therefore can subjugate and even murder entire groups not belonging to their group. This is taking a fundamental wrong view and acting in an extreme way.

We may not be overtly elitist, but we may still possess the *view of superiority*—instinctively considering some to be inferior to us and others to be superior. Even a seemingly positive emotion like pity can come from a sense of superiority. So we must be careful.

Views that regard unsatisfactory moral and spiritual disciplines as supreme are powerful influences in our world today, as we can see in the growth of fanaticism and religious intolerance. There are many spiritual practitioners who feel that their path is the only true path and that all others are inferior or wrong. I see this in a secular context, too. Living in England, which is not a religious country, I come across many who feel that people with religious convictions are brainwashed, stupid, and superstitious. Some circles consider a cynical and irreligious perspective uniquely superior.

Many people who have a corporate job, wear a suit, carry a briefcase, and drive a car feel that their lifestyle is superior to others and that those trying to follow a spiritual path are only doing so because they cannot succeed in business. This view is very persuasive because it pervades our culture, but really, it is just a secular version of regarding unsatisfactory ethics as supreme.

From a Buddhist perspective, *wrong view* is either believing nonexistent things to exist, or conversely believing that existent things don't exist. For example, a person might have strong anger at either himself or others, but feel that it is reasonable because no negative consequences will result from that anger, or if they do they will be negligible. That person will have no thought of long-term consequences at all, their wrong view based on the assumption that nothing exists beyond the surface world of sensory consciousness. Conversely, a person might perceive something to exist that does not, such as someone who hallucinates from taking drugs feeling that the hallucination is real.

Within Buddhism, the big debate focuses not around anger or hallucinations, but the sense of "I" or self. Those who feel the "I" does not exist at all, or that it does exist, but intrinsically, independent of the mind/body aggregates, are said to hold wrong views.

True awareness of the relationship between cause and effect is the antidote to these views. Even if we meet very charismatic people who try to convince us that their philosophy is superior to all others, or that the views of others are completely mistaken, with an understanding of cause and effect we will be able to differentiate for ourselves what is right and wrong. Any practice that helps us decrease selfish concern will lead to more skillful and accurate views.

The Third Zone

The derivative mental afflictions in the third zone arise in dependence on our physical nervous system and our social situation—meaning the society we are brought up in or the environment around us. While the mental factors of the second zone are said to be *more* gross than those in the first zone, those of the third zone are said to be *very* gross in their expression and function compared with the other zones. However, they might still be too subtle to distinguish without investigation.

In the third zone, we find mindstates with which most of us are familiar. In the chart they are arranged in the five traditional groups,[16] although I have added some that are not traditionally included within the fifty-one mental factors. I am sure you could extent this list indefinitely!

Categorizing these factors into five groups is mostly to enhance our grasp of the factors; the categories are not rigid and are in fact very much interrelated. A mental factor from one group can trigger one from another. Vengeful feelings could arise from the anger we feel when somebody hurts us, but it might equally arise from attachment or from jealousy. This example should remind us that our emotions are complex and messy, and their classification is a very indefinite science.

LOOKING AT INDIVIDUAL MENTAL FACTORS

The five boxes in the third zone merely show the immediate causes of our strongest delusions in a very general way. For instance, self-satisfaction and excitement arise from attachment—that is fairly obvious—but so too do anxiety and fear of loss. It is worth investigating these patterns in your own lives to see if they hold true for you.

Some of the mental factors labeled *derived from all three main mental afflictions* are interesting to look at. What is the difference between pretension and shamelessness? Pretension arises from a strong sense of ego. It is a sense of superiority that discounts other people's feelings, which is one of the main obstacles to developing compassion. Shamelessness, on the other hand, is of lack of consideration for ourselves. This is a very dangerous mental factor. With shamelessness, we follow whatever arises in our mental continuum without concern for the consequences. This makes us capable of great harm. Some modern Abhidharma scholars use Hitler to exemplify this point.

Among the mental factors caused by *attachment and ignorance*, prejudice, for example, contains an element of anger, but its main components are ignorance and attachment. It is ignorance because it sees another as intrinsically inferior or separate. It is attachment because someone with prejudice fears losing his or her identity or some perceived advantage. Racial prejudice can be caused by many different factors and itself can trigger other minds, such as disrespect, hatred, and cruelty. Pride, self-grasping, and self-hatred can also fuel racism.

In some ways the minds derived from ignorance alone are the most difficult to handle. These mental factors—such as dullness, forgetfulness, and laziness—cause the mind to lose its energy, clarity, and intensity, without which we are incapable of the action necessary to deal with the problem. Pride and anger, in contrast, do not lack intensity. While still destructive, they can be more easily transformed because they are active mindstates analyzed by active mindstates. We can see not only how they are negative but also (hopefully) how we can eliminate them.

Grief is included within the minds that are deadening and therefore difficult to counteract because of their lack of intensity. This might seem strange to you, for isn't grief a powerful mind? It can be. On the one hand, the fundamental emotions that underlie grief are confusion and pointlessness, which are linked to dullness. When the World Trade Center was destroyed by terrorists, many people said they felt "flat" and directionless for days. Only later did the many other complex emotions arise. That flatness is grief. On the other hand, grief is often closely linked to attachment. We were attached to someone or something that is now gone. These examples demonstrate the complexity of the mental factors and how they function in our minds.

How the Derivative Mental Afflictions Arise

Although the mental events that we are experiencing now derive from the gross afflictions charted in the third zone, they are also related to previous causes. On one level, these afflictions are conditioned by our environment, family situation, and education. Someone from a dysfunctional family or someone with no education is less likely to be able to control the anger and frustrations that arise in everyday life. If we examine with an understanding of the Dharma, however, we can see that the conditions of our environment, family, and education are themselves products of the actions we performed in previous lives.

Stress and depression are related to the pressures of modern society, but ignorance is the root cause. If we work so hard that there is not enough time to relax, we may well become stressed and depressed. We think affluence is the route to happiness, but obtaining it can be so stressful that we make ourselves totally depressed and unhappy. To me, this reflects a gross level of ignorance. If we were free of ignorance, however, we could work all day and all night and never become stressed out. So the main cause of stress is ignorance.

It is the same with other forms of ignorance. Tobacco addiction combines a physical addiction with a gross mental longing. Despite knowing the damage being done, a heavy smoker continues to smoke. In fact, most of us have addictions of some kind. My addiction is watching television, despite knowing that it is a waste of time and bad for my eyes. But these examples are very gross, and these obsessions—these mental events—do not arise from our previous lives; my bad habits were not built up from lifetimes of watching television!

Why does an alcoholic, for example, continue to drink even though he intellectually understands that drinking causes him to make a mess of his life and destroy his body? Something, some mental factor, pushes him to keep drinking. Perhaps if this person's intellectual understanding penetrated in a deep, heartfelt way, he might develop the conviction to make a lasting change. It is the same with samsara in general—only when we truly see the defects of contaminated happiness on a gut level can we develop the will to seek complete liberation.

Every action of body, speech, or mind leaves an imprint on our mindstream and has the potential to create a habit. Small habits grow into large ones—social drinking can lead to alcoholism, disregard for small lives, such as insects, can lead to abuse and even homicide. These things come from not understanding the gross level of cause and effect. When a person is already an alcoholic, the addiction is very difficult to break; so habitual tendencies need to be detected and addressed as early as possible.

At the moment we might not have strong anger or racial prejudice, but this does not mean we are totally free of the problems listed under the heading of *ignorance of the gross relationship of the law of cause and effect*. Perhaps our lives look very good at present—we are not depressed, we have a new job and plenty of money in the bank. However, as long as we have this fundamental ignorance (first zone), we have the potential to develop selfish concern (second zone). With selfish concern it is all too easy to experience the disappointment, anger, and frustration that will then lead to depression. It is wise to not be complacent, but analyze the states of mind we experience and trace them back to their causes.

One important thing that will arise from this kind of analysis is the understanding that our states of mind are *not* primarily caused by external conditions. We might feel hopeless that our lives are a mess, or we might feel great grief because of the death of a loved one, but these external events are just conditions that have triggered our state of mind; the main cause is internal.

In our lives, we continually misconceive reality—we take to heart everything that society considers important and feel either that we are not getting enough, or that what we have is not good enough. We easily become jealous or competitive. It is not difficult to get wrapped up in this kind of vicious circle. Look around you at all those people who are obsessed with status and possessions—the big house, the expensive car. Health is also important, but so many people now spend huge sums of money to work out in expensive gyms. When we misconceive reality it is very easy to become obsessed. And then, when our obsession lets us down, which will definitely happen sooner or later, we will experience anger and depression.

4 DEALING WITH NEGATIVE EMOTIONS

IN DEALING WITH THE DISTURBING MENTAL FACTORS that bring us suffering, we may encounter a seemingly unbridgeable gap between theory and practice, especially with overwhelming emotions like anger or depression. We might see the wisdom in looking deep within our minds for the answer to our problems, but we may also feel totally overwhelmed by emotion. Then we may think, "My anger at *that* person *now* is all I can really deal with." In fact, this is the very state of mind with which we should begin. For ultimately, only our internal resources—our love, patience, tolerance, and understanding—will lift us from our negative states and bring us deep and lasting happiness.

We can begin by examining whatever afflictive emotion is plaguing us right now and seeing it for what it is. I will use anger as my primary example, because it is a very common negative mental state and one of the most damaging. What follows, however, can apply to any mental affliction.[17]

Anger is a negative emotion. It is unhealthy and causes so many problems. Therefore, the first thing to do is convince yourself deeply that anger is undesirable by contemplating the faults of anger. If you are not firmly convinced that anger is a problem, you won't apply yourself to getting rid of it. You do this is by reviewing all the ways that anger destroys your mental health, your physical well-being, and your sleep, on the one hand, and how it leads to harmful actions of body and speech on the other hand, endangering the safety and welfare of those around you and bringing intense suffering in future lives. Once you see how devastating the effects of anger are, then you need to find ways to reduce and finally eliminate it.

Anger is actually fairly easy to get rid of because its negative effects are so obvious. The afflictive emotions that come from attachment are more insidious, because they can appear to make us happy. Thus, the analysis of their drawbacks is crucial. We have to see precisely how craving, for instance, leads to negative actions, harming ourselves and those around us, and blocking us from liberation. If you truly grasp the drawbacks of the mental afflictions on a deep level, then abandoning them becomes relatively easy. They will appear to you, as Lama Zopa says, like used toilet paper.

It is important to recognize that all mental events, from niggling irritation to all-consuming hatred, are impermanent. It might seem that they are a permanent aspect of our psyche because they have accompanied us for so long, but there is nothing eternal about them. Anger, for instance, may be so ingrained and operating on so many levels of our mind that eliminating it seems hopeless. While there is no shortcut, there *is* a definite route to liberation from our negative states of mind—provided we are persistent and apply the right effort to right method.

Whatever negative mindset we have, the key is to view it as nothing more than an internal emotion. If we do that, we shift the focus from the external object that seems to be causing the anger onto the internal problem. Rather than destroying the object of anger—our "enemy"—we target and finally eliminate the mind of anger. That transformative dimension is paramount in Buddhism and is what gives Buddhism an edge over many other philosophies. For if a problem is within our own mind, then we have the power to change it. We don't need to rely on anyone else or on some external change.

When we are lost in our anger, we need to broaden our minds. It only *seems* the worst thing that has ever happened because we are fused with it. If we step back, we can see our pattern, and realize that our anger is related more to our mind's habits than to the actual person or event causing *this* particular incident. We can never stop external things from happening, but we can change the way we react to them by looking beyond the external causes—the thoughtless boss, the noisy neighbor—and examine why anger arises when such circumstances are present.

In the fifth chapter of *Guide to a Bodhisattva's Way of Life*, the eighth-century Indian yogi Shantideva says:

> Where would I possibly find enough leather
> With which to cover the surface of the earth?
> But (wearing) leather just on the soles of my shoes
> Is equivalent to covering the earth with it.[18]

Of course it is ridiculous to think that we can render the earth harmless by covering it with leather. And yet this is exactly what we attempt to do in relation to our external environment—manipulate it in order to bring about out own happiness, which is impossible. As in Shantideva's example, the best we can do to protect our feet is cover them with shoes, and the best we can do to protect our own happiness is change our minds so that we no longer perceive a particular set of circumstances as a problem. Controlling our minds in this way is like buying it a pair of shoes—protecting it from the sharp thorns of our external conditions.

There is no way we can force all beings to be our friends, nor can we demand that everyone be sweet and generous. However, by transforming our minds, we can free ourselves from dependence on external conditions. That freedom, in turn, allows us to assess other peoples' situations honestly, and compassion toward them will naturally arise. We will see them as friends, regardless of how they treat us. Therefore, if we address the anger and aversion within ourselves, our problems will diminish and slowly disappear. Let us look at this process more closely.

THE CAUSE OF ANGER

Imagine a difficult situation that you are likely to encounter in the near future, one that involves a person who knows just how to push your buttons. Then, imagine the probable consequence—you get angry. From the safe distance of your imagination, explore the effects of this anger. It is not too difficult to see that it is much better to avoid losing your temper and find other ways of handling the situation. Of course, confronting a troublesome situation in the imagination is much easier than in real life, but with practice, over time, your reaction to a recurring difficult situation can change, and you can start to manage it skillfully.

With awareness and a bit of distance, you can look objectively at why anger arises in the first place. This means looking beyond the immediate conditions to the main cause. Perhaps your teenage son has taken the car without permission and crashed it. It's difficult not to get angry! But that situation is not the *cause* of your anger. If car crashes involving teenagers truly caused you anger, you would be angry on countless occasions every day. The accident is not the cause of your anger, but it is one of the conditions that has triggered it. First, he is *your* son, and the situation exposes the complexities of your parent-child relationship. You may have observed your son's behavior becoming more and more out of control in the last few months, and you feel that his friends are a bad influence. You may be thinking of the expense and inconvenience of repairing the car. You may be in shock about the injury he could have sustained. These are all conditions, but the root cause is much more profound.

Abhidharma texts cite three conditions that trigger an afflictive emotion:

1. We have not abandoned afflictive emotions.
2. We remain close to the object of our afflictive emotion.
3. We still have distorted emotions.

Not having abandoned afflictive emotions, their seeds are always present in us, ready to ripen. In this vulnerable state, we get too close to whatever conditions cause them to arise. Without any distance from the object disturbing us, we have no way to explore the causes objectively. The last condition, distorted emotion, is the simple fact that we have little control over our emotions and we superimpose these distortions onto reality. When these three conditions come together, there is no way we can stop anger, or jealousy, or whatever afflictive emotion is poised to arise in our minds.

Sooner or later we must skillfully confront each of these three conditions. Perhaps at this stage it is impossible to address our distorted emotion directly—that negative mind is bubbling away no matter what we do—and of course the root cause is too deep. So maybe we need to distance ourselves from the object of the afflicted emotion—the person who brings out our bad side or the substance we're addicted to. Without that distance, we may have no opportunity to penetrate the emotional smokescreen and get at the actual causes of our negativity.

Ultimately, what we will find is that the cause of our problems is not our boss, the government, or our partner, but the deep-seated discontent in our minds. Anger is not something external, out there—it is an internal state of mind, and so we should seek its causes inside ourselves.

Based on discontent, which itself arises from our fundamental confusion, anger breeds further confusion. This is why Buddhism says that anger is *always* negative—because its long-term results are always suffering. Although we may feel that anger can bring short-term satisfaction, in reality an outburst of anger leaves an imprint on our mindstream that puts us in grave danger. And once it arises, that makes it more likely to arise again, until a habit is formed. The more angry we get, the more habituated to anger we become.

When we confront anger, we should keep in mind that the anger we feel is not the entire sum of our consciousness but is in fact only a part of our mindstream. True, it might be dominant at the moment, and it might seem that we are nothing more than our anger, but was it there yesterday? Will that same anger relating to that same object be present next week? If we are honest, the answer is no. Separating our sense of self from the transient and partial emotion we call anger, we gain distance and are better able to confront it.

ANGER AND LOGIC

At the moment, rather than addressing the main cause of anger, most of us are continuously caught up in its contributing factors. In this situation, logic can be dangerous. Often we use logic to reason out a justifiable (but incorrect) premise for our anger, sit on it for days, review the scenario repeatedly, and talk ourselves into a true state of hatred. I am not suggesting that negative things do not happen and that everything is all just a projection. People do act negatively toward us. However, we should be very wary of black-and-white interpretations. Whenever we feel we are completely in the right and the other person is completely in the wrong, we should be aware that that is probably a very biased interpretation.

Although the faulty logic we use to justify our anger should be avoided, if we are skillful we can use logic as a tool for getting out of our negative emotion. On the one hand, anger is an emotion that is very difficult to handle. On the other hand, the intellectual justifications we dream up are cognitive constructs, and these can be analyzed intellectually with success. By observing the fundamental irrationality of blaming the other person, the mind that seeks to justify our anger is defused. When anger about the situation arises again, we use that same logic to counteract our habitual story. Over and over again, we repeatedly use the skillful logic to counteract the logic of the afflictive emotion. Starved of its justification, our anger will diminish over time.

We should be aware of the role that intellectual justification plays in developing, sustaining, and increasing anger. We may think that anger is just pure emotion, but anger always has a cognitive aspect—a rhetoric that drives it. On a collective level, groups—even whole nations—can be roused to hatred by argument. Racial prejudice, and at its worst, ethnic cleansing, are fueled by rhetoric. On a much smaller scale, we fuel our own anger when we replay the soap opera of the argument again and again, justifying ourselves as right and our enemy as wrong.

Anger never consists of pure emotion devoid of logic. It is never just "I hate you!" but always "I hate you because..." We interpret every situation we confront. If incorrect interpretation is possible, which is what happens we are really angry, then the possibility for correct interpretation should also exist. We cannot transform the blind emotion of anger, but we can work on the mistaken concepts that fuel and justify it. We can begin this transformation right now, while we have some distance from that emotion and the constructs that accompany it.

MEDITATING ON ANGER

Suppressing anger, or any other afflictive emotion, only leads to an explosion down the road. We need to defuse it so that it does not arise again. This is best done in meditation when we are feeling calm and rational.

When I was in the monastery we had no alarm clocks. Rising late was awful—not just because we would have to enter the hall in the middle of prayers, but more crucially because we would miss out on that very important morning cup of tea! Very early on we all trained ourselves to awaken at the proper time by repeating the hour over and over again to ourselves. It's amazing how you can habituate your mind to anything. Effective meditation is powerful because it creates an ideal laboratory for rewiring our mental processes.

You only become convinced of the disadvantages of anger when you explore them repeatedly. Then your attitude begins to change. This process can only occur within the framework of meditation. Hearing or reading about the disadvantages of anger might convince you intellectually, but it will have little effect on your ability to actually confront it. Only when you are deeply convinced that anger itself, not external forces, is your enemy, will you be motivated to actually turn things around. With a really strong conviction, it is surprisingly easy to avoid the outer manifestations of anger and, in time, the actual angry mind.

Eventually, the awareness of the disadvantages of anger you are building up in moments of calm will slowly seep down into your emotional life. Things that previously would trigger your anger instead trigger a caution that anger might arise, and you will be on guard against it. In Tibetan we say, "Build the dike before the water comes." If you know the river will flood, prepare your defenses beforehand.

Another way to meditate on anger is to replay scenes in which you have been angry before, using the distance and clarity of a calm, meditative mind. This does not mean replaying the movie and getting angry all over again! You are not doing this to convince yourselves how unjust that other person was. You are recollecting the suffering that anger has brought you. You can also ponder how you might have handled the situation had anger not dictated your behavior. In the laboratory of the meditative mind, make various experiments and find out what is best for you and for others.

As with an addiction, when you have overcome an afflictive emotion like anger, you will see the destruction it has brought into your life and how it has enslaved you.

DEVELOPING EQUANIMITY

An important aspect of our current negative mindset is our lack of equanimity. We judge people all the time, putting them in our "friend" or our "enemy" box, or simply ignoring them because they have nothing to offer us. We all see things from a fairly narrow perspective; life is too busy and complex to have the space to take everything in, and our minds become selective. We tend to undervalue people. We see them not as they really are but in terms of how they relate to us and serve—or thwart—our needs. Therefore, when someone hinders us in some way—say they cut us off in traffic or criticize us in public—we see that person as a hindrance. Stuck in that perception, we condemn a person on the basis of this or that *bad* personality trait—the trait that blocks them from seeing how important we are. Of course, they wouldn't see it that way!

If we never perceive people as more than objects in the game of making "me" happy, then we will always have huge problems. We need not know all other people in their entirety to progress from this narrow worldview. In Buddhism we do this by cultivating equanimity.

Beneath the surface, everyone is motivated by a wish to be happy and to avoid suffering. In this sense, all are equal. This equality goes beyond color, race, sex, or personality to the actual inner life of beings. There is no difference whatsoever between any of us at this deeper level.

If we can cultivate this understanding of the basic equality of all beings, then we can start to see potential problems more objectively. Not only is my enemy's opinion equally valid, but also his needs and rights are equally valid. I am angry because he is blocking my happiness in some way, but isn't that the same for him? And he has exactly the same right to happiness as I have.

We don't usually feel compassion for people on a holiday, do we? When others are going to the beach, sailing a big yacht, and working on a suntan, it can be hard to feel any sympathy for them—in fact we might feel quite envious. This shows that we have not understood that all people, in time, experience the full range of physical and mental suffering. In fact, someone on a tropical beach may be suffering more on a mental level than someone on an assembly line.

Only with the impartial compassion that arises from equanimity can we collapse our "friend," "enemy," and "stranger" boxes forever. This is the mind that we must try to develop.

Offering the Victory to Others

We can take this even further. Rather than just observe that others have an equal right to happiness, we can take the next step and actually put our own happiness aside for their sakes. Actually, this method is the only way we will ever achieve true happiness.

Imagine that someone has done me great harm for no apparent reason. How should I handle this situation? Normally, I might take revenge—I might plot to harm him back. What result does that bring? I suffer even more and so does he.

But perhaps I can see the disadvantages of retaliation, so I stop myself. Instead, I silently hate him. That is a better solution but still inadequate. Perhaps I come to forgive him but still do not understand him. This is better still, but a long way from turning the situation into a positive one.

One profound Buddhist technique is to offer the victory to your enemy. This may seem very unnatural, but it is possible and can bring amazing results. This practice has nothing to do with being a doormat. What it means is that instead of trying to cause harm to someone who has harmed you, you do completely the opposite and actually try to help that person. This is the victory, because it becomes the cause of happiness for both of you.

In *Guide to a Bodhisattva's Way of Life*, Shantideva says:

> The victorious warriors are those
> Who, having disregarded all suffering,
> Vanquish the foes of hatred and so forth;
> (Common warriors) slay only corpses.[19]

This is an amazing way to look at things, isn't it? In a normal battle, we have to sacrifice many things and suffer a great deal to gain victory over our external enemies. Here, Shantideva reveals our real enemies—anger, vengeance, vindictiveness, and so on—and instructs us to destroy these minds, not the external enemy. If we manage this, we will naturally help both ourselves and the person causing us problems.

DEVELOPING PATIENCE

Buddhism suggests two main antidotes to anger: patience and love. Standing at a wet bus stop for hours and hating it is not really patience. To practice patience, in addition to physically enduring a difficult situation, we need to have a content mind.

You might wonder why anyone would *willingly* endure suffering in the first place. The explanation is very simple—in this life, no one escapes suffering. Since we all have to endure it, why compound it by developing a negative mind about it? Feeling content even though the bus has not come is better than feeling angry about it. Either way you are still wet and waiting for that bus.

This should not be taken to mean that we should be masochists, seeking out misery and making ourselves suffer, or that we dumbly acquiesce to suffering when it happens. Do what you need to, but don't let your mind get upset about your situation. Shantideva gives the simplest but most profound advice on this:

Why be unhappy about something
If it can be remedied?
And what is the use of being unhappy about something
If it cannot be remedied?[20]

In this practice, self-awareness is vital. Without knowing we are suffering, we will have no desire to change it; and without knowing the roots of that suffering, we will have no means to change it. This leads us back to the issue of the correct interpretation of the event. Obviously, if we can do nothing about a late bus, we must endure the wait.

Of course this practice is more difficult when the situation is more dramatic—for example, if someone is being deliberately malicious. Suppose someone is vandalizing our property or is insulting us behind our back. We can interpret the situation in many ways. We can think, this person hates me, is harming me deliberately, and this is entirely her choice—the situation is completely under her control. This is the way the angry mind usually interprets a situation of this kind. To the angry mind there is never any justification for "her" actions and always plenty justification for "mine."

However, there is another choice here. We can think, "I am acting unskillfully because I am controlled by my anger. Maybe it is the same with the other person. Maybe she is controlled by emotions and is suffering just as much as I am. And further, maybe I have contributed to the situation in some way and I am at least partially responsible. If I really were as perfect as my wounded ego is telling me I am, then there would be no way that person could upset me so much. So maybe I need to look at exactly why I am so upset from the point of view of my own shortcomings rather than hers." A thought process along these lines can help us diffuse the anger in our minds.

If we see a seriously unstable man inflicting injuries on himself, we readily admit that he is out of control and does not realize what he is doing. This is an extreme example, but really, in everyday life, none of us are totally aware of what we are doing. Just as we are driven by irrational rage and the wish to retaliate when someone hurts us, so that person who harms us is driven by forces outside of his control. He is the instrument of his disturbed emotions in the same way that we are when we get angry.

Thinking like this, we can insert a gap between the situation and our minds. In that gap, patience will grow. Shantideva uses the analogy of being beaten with a stick to illustrate the dependent nature of all our actions.

If I become angry with the wielder
Although I am actually harmed by the stick,

> Then since the perpetrator, too, is secondary, being in turn
> incited by hatred,
> I should be angry with his hatred instead.[21]

Getting angry at the stick is illogical, but if we examine it, so too is getting angry at the person, who, ruled by his negative emotions, is just as much a passive instrument as the stick. Seeing how both parties in the argument are equally out of control, we can develop empathy for our adversary. This is the start of patience.

Taking this even further, the transformation really starts, and we actively begin to learn to endure suffering willingly. If we really analyze a situation, we will find that it is not completely negative. No matter how bad things are, we can always learn something. What we can learn is patience, which, from a Buddhist point of view, is one of the most important qualities to develop. So this unpleasant experience, if used properly, can actually enrich and ennoble our lives.

How many people have admitted they have grown through unpleasant experiences? In Buddhism we say that your friends do not help you develop because they cater to your sense of self, whereas an enemy challenges your sense of self, and so is uniquely capable of showing you your weaknesses. In that way your worst enemy is your best friend—if you can use him or her that way!

If we perceive a difficult event as something positive, it will be less painful, and there will be less suffering. I'm always amazed when I watch the London marathon. All those thousands of people going through all that suffering—willingly! They see something very positive happening, and so they undertake all that pain with joy. For me, it would be sheer misery. But difficult situations are only negative if we allow them to be problems.

DEVELOPING LOVE

The opposite of hatred is love, and love is the best antidote to anger. Our anger can only be directed at one of three objects: ourselves, other beings, or inanimate objects such as things, events, and ideas. Besides huge ideologies, which can be objects of intense hatred, it is usually fairly easy to deal with our feelings in relation to objects because there is no emotional interaction. Although maybe I should exclude computers from that statement! Generally, however, our greatest difficulties are with living beings, ourselves or others.

Start with yourself. To meditate on giving yourself love, you first need to acknowledge that you are not happy. Whether due to a deprived childhood, a frustrated ambition, or relationship problems, you are hard on yourself and lack something you really want—love. And so, in meditation, you recognize this, and without dwelling on the causes too much, you imagine bright white light at your heart, spreading out and filling your whole being with light and love. Doing this often will slowly lighten your anguish and give you space to explore the reasons you feel hollow or angry, and the methods to overcome it.

It is exactly the same process when you want to feel love toward others. Whether a person who has given you difficulties, a stranger you have heard about who is really suffering, or a group of friends, the process is to acknowledge that they are suffering and then, with all your heart, wish them sincere and lasting happiness. Imagine how freeing it would feel if you could genuinely wish your worst enemy happiness! That dark, heavy weight at your heart would lift immediately. So, in the same way, imagine a bright white light at your heart, only this time it shoots out like a laser beam and enters the person or people you are meditating on and fills them with white light, resulting in their happiness.

Love, according to Buddhism, is wishing someone to be happy. It is nothing more than that. It is not attachment or lust; it is a simple and beautiful emotion.

Compassion is the other side of the coin. Everyone wants to have happiness and to avoid suffering, so love is wishing them happiness and compassion is wishing them to be free from suffering. With compassion, the focus is not on the happiness we wish for ourselves or others, but on the suffering we and others are filled with at present. In this meditation you make yourself aware of that suffering and then sincerely aspire to eliminate it. Other than that, the meditation is the same, with white light filling the person's being (or your own body, if you are concentrating on yourself) and eliminating every atom of suffering.

Focusing on the person who is making you angry is a wonderful meditation. Imagine all the good qualities that that person has in potential, and imagine as you fill him or her with white light that those qualities are actualized. Sometimes it may be emotionally painful to do this with an enemy, but it is painful in a positive way.

There is no magic trick to ridding ourselves of negative emotions. We must confront and overcome them through internal analysis and meditation and with a great deal of patience; it is a slow process. Realizing the destructive nature of the negative emotions, such as anger, and understanding that their causes always lie latent in our minds, we begin the practice of reducing them and lessening their influence in our lives.

5 WHOLESOME MENTAL FACTORS

THE THREE FUNDAMENTAL POSITIVE MENTAL FACTORS

OF THE SIX CATEGORIES OF MENTAL FACTORS, we have dealt with the always-present, the object-ascertaining, and the negative mental factors and have briefly mentioned the variable mental factors. That leaves us with the ones we want to develop—the positive or wholesome mental factors. In the traditional list, eleven wholesome mental factors are mentioned, but I have elaborated on these to highlight their varying degrees of subtlety. As with the negative mental factors, I have categorized them into three zones.

At the core of our psyche are three wholesome mental factors: nonattachment, nonhatred, and nonignorance. These root virtuous mindstates belong to zone 1. They exist in the mind as potentials and as subterranean forces; they only manifest directly when we peel back the onion skins of increasingly more subtle minds to reveal them.

As was the case with negative mental factors, we need to deal first with the least-subtle ones of zone 3, although here of course we are trying to develop the positive mindstates rather than eliminate the negative ones. Before we can develop compassion, for example, we need a degree of equanimity and mindfulness. Although the positive mental factors of the third zone can counteract third-zone negative mental factors, they do not effectively manage the negative mental factors that are more deep-rooted. For example, friendliness or a calm state of mind are not real antidotes to our self-centered attitudes.

WHOLESOME MENTAL FACTORS

mental factors	aspect of noble eightfold path
THIRD ZONE	
• confidence • optimism • joy • equanimity • friendliness • calmness • mindfulness • correct understanding of cause and effect	• right effort • right action • right speech • right livelihood
SECOND ZONE	
• loving-kindness • compassion • altruism • calm abiding • constant mindfulness of body, speech, and mind • constant application to long-term goals	• right mindfulness • right concentration
FIRST ZONE	
• nonattachment • nonhatred • nonignorance	• right thought • right view

Nonattachment, the first wholesome mental factor in zone 1, is the opposite of attachment. Whereas attachment exaggerates the qualities of an object, nonattachment sees how external conditions are unreliable sources of pleasure. Suppose you possess a beautiful object, an antique. Through examination of its parts and its impermanence, you can come to understand its nature. With such objects, worldly people focus on how expensive it is or how much other people admire it. Through investigation, you can come to see the flip side—that no matter how beautiful or valuable the object is, it has the potential to bring suffering. Understanding this deeply plants the seeds of nonattachment.

Every object that brings us pleasure can also bring us suffering and anxiety. The more we value an object, the more we worry that it will be broken or taken from us. That is the nature of our mind and of our relationship with objects.

It is possible to develop nonattachment even to our own bodies. That does not mean we neglect our bodies or health. But through examining the nature of our bodies, and understanding that they are composed merely of flesh, bones, skin, organs, and so on, nonattachment naturally grows.

The nature of the body is also one of continual change. I have a photo of myself in boarding school at nine years old. My hands were so small, but now they are huge; and my skin was so smooth, but now it's quite rough. I now have wrinkles and gray hair. These are gross changes, but even on a subtle level my body is undergoing continual change. Although my body is not bringing me great suffering at the moment, that potential is there. Examining in this way, an understanding of the nature of things will arise, and nonattachment will develop naturally.

Nonattachment is also called detachment, but I feel this term can be misleading, suggesting a mild form of aversion that is not in operation here. Nonattachment is simply knowing the nature of the object and, as a result, not following our normal clinging in relation to it. Nonattachment is not a state of no feeling. It is a fully functioning mindstate that does not cling, grasp, or want more.

In the same way, *nonhatred* is one of the core qualities of our minds. When we say our mind is free from hatred, what is present is a complete lack of discrimination—seeing some sentient beings as friends, some as enemies, and some as strangers. This mental factor is endowed with the quality of love for ourselves and for others, without bias. It understands other beings' sufferings as well as their genuine happiness. Nonhatred is the greatest quality of mind we can possess. We will experience real peace of mind only when nonhatred is developed.

Nonignorance is a synonym for wisdom. It refers to freedom from the fundamental confusion that functions at the deepest, most subtle level of mind. Nonignorance, like the other root virtuous mental factors, it is not passive, but endowed with clear and active wisdom and understanding.

In this context *wisdom* refers to the understanding of how things and events actually exist. By starting with a conceptual understanding, and then developing qualities such as single-pointed concentration and compassion, the mind can be led to a direct realization of the true nature of all phenomena. Only then will the most fundamental confusion, ignorance, be eliminated.

The Traditional Eleven Positive Mental Factors

While these three root mental factors are the core of the positive mind, other virtuous mental states are also considered vital. Traditionally, Buddhist scholars list eleven root positive mental factors:

1. nonattachment

2. nonhatred

3. nonignorance

4. faith

5. self-respect

6. consideration for others

7. enthusiasm

8. suppleness

9. conscientiousness

10. equanimity

11. nonviolence

It's not difficult to understand how important these are.

Take faith, for example. *Faith* in Buddhism does not refer to blind faith, but to faith that arises from observation and reflection. The Buddha's teachings include things too subtle for us to fully comprehend at this time, such as the most intricate workings of karma. But because we can prove the logical truth of what the Buddha says about things we *can* check up on, such as momentary impermanence, we can develop conviction that the more subtle teachings are also correct.

Self-worth and *consideration for others* are two sides of the same coin, and both are crucial to our development. They are similar in that they inspire us to refrain from harmful actions—toward ourselves in the case of self-worth, and toward others in the case of consideration for others. How can we develop our minds if we are plagued by low self-esteem, which is as unrealistic and ego-driven as arrogance? And how can we help others if we have no consideration for their perspective or well-being?

As a support for spiritual development, we need to increase our mental capacity through meditation. Specifically, we need to cultivate equanimity, conscientiousness, and suppleness. *Equanimity* here refers to a stable mind, free of excitement or dullness. The other type of equanimity we often speak of—regarding all beings as equal in their right to have happiness and avoid suffering—is just as important. *Conscientiousness* and suppleness are crucial to clarity. Conscientiousness is related to joyous perseverance, the energy that allows us to undertake difficult (and sometimes seemingly thankless) work to help others, and one of the six perfections of a bodhisattva. *Suppleness* in this context does not refer to suppleness of body but of mind— meaning that flexibility that allows the mind to overcome obstacles to meditation and positive action. At present we want to practice, but we face obstacles—the mind is tight or agitated, or we read a passage a dozen times and still can't understand it. This rigidity that arises from past negative habits is overcome by suppleness.

The last mind, *nonviolence*, is one much discussed these days, with champions such as Gandhi and His Holiness the Dalai Lama showing by their example that this practice is the only way to avoid the conflicts that we usually consider inevitable. Nonviolence can be applied to all levels of our lives, however; we should not consider it merely physical. We also need to restrain from mental violence—the wish to harm others—and verbal violence, harming others through our speech. The great contemporary Buddhist master, Thich Nhat Hanh, says that even drinking a cup of tea without mindfulness is an act of violence! Geshe Rabten equates nonviolence with compassion, and that is equally valid.[22]

The Pyramid of the Three Trainings

Developing wholesome mental factors requires the complete transformation of our current negative mental states. In his teaching on the four noble truths, the Buddha presents the blueprint to achieve this, the noble eightfold path, which itself encompasses the three trainings of ethics, concentration, and wisdom.

Although traditionally illustrated by the Dharma wheel, the three trainings can also be represented as a pyramid. The base of the pyramid is ethics, upon which the two sides of the pyramid rest—one side is meditation or concentration, and the other is insight or wisdom. Meditation and wisdom can only stand upright upon the base of ethics. In reality, all three are mutually dependent. Without meditation, wisdom is dry and intellectual and ethics are tight and lifeless; without wisdom, meditation progresses slowly and ethics are clumsily applied. We need not have the direct understanding of emptiness for it to benefit our practice; just reminding ourselves that everything is changeable and interdependent can enrich meditation and increase the motivation to act in an ethical way.

What do we speak of when we speak of ethics? One aspect of ethics is the rules of discipline for different levels of Buddhist teachings. In this context, however, we are speaking of ethics in terms of the commonsense morality—caring for one's fellow beings and foregoing harm—that is characteristic of every society and religion. Buddhism has many ways of enumerating those actions to adopt and those to avoid, but they all boil down to benefiting others and refraining from harm.

The second of the three trainings, concentration, is crucial to leading a wholesome life. Concentration not only focuses the mind to help it penetrate the deeper views of reality, it also gives rise to physical pleasure and makes the mind more emotionally balanced. Many of the people who come to the Dharma center in London are slowly turning away from the frantic pace that city life demands and creating the space to follow a spiritual path. Stepping out of the whirlwind is the first step to developing a more focused mind, and the basis for future training in the more refined states such as calm abiding (Skt. *shamata*, Tib. *shiné*), a deep mental stability that can be sustained effortlessly for long periods of time.

Again, the third training, wisdom, need not be developed through formal Buddhist study. People who have well-developed knowledge of other technical disciplines often take easily to the precise explanations of emptiness given in the texts. A good store of practical wisdom—the understanding of appropriate behavior and of how the world works—can also take us far. The more profound and subtle levels of wisdom, such as the understanding of selflessness and the realization of emptiness, will build on these.

In general, negative emotion is spontaneous. It can arise without apparent reason, sometimes so strongly it is impossible to control. Wisdom, on the other hand, ripens slowly in dependence on rational analysis and meditative stability. Thus, we need to employ the tools of both the experiential and the intellectual aspects of our minds to attain our goals, with ethics as our base.

Positive Mental Factors in the Second Zone

THE NOBLE EIGHTFOLD PATH IN THE THREE ZONES

Mental factors that are less subtle than the three root wholesome ones, but probably still too subtle to be perceived, can be placed in the second zone of increasing subtlety. They are: loving-kindness, altruism, compassion, constant mindfulness, constant application to long-term goals, and calm abiding.

Nonattachment, nonhatred, and nonignorance are a long way off. They are the qualities that will shine through when we have eliminated all the unwholesome mindstates that currently cloud our minds. To do that the Buddha explained the path we each must take, the eightfold noble path. The aspects of the path related to verbal or physical actions—right effort, right speech, right action, and right livelihood—are antidotes to the unwholesome mental factors in the third zone. The mental factors related to the other four aspects belong in the subtler zones 1 and 2. We can place right mindfulness and right concentration in zone 2 and right view and right thought—the most subtle aspects of the path—in zone 1.

With right effort, right speech, right action, and right livelihood we are trying to restrain from wrong actions and perform virtuous ones. With right mindfulness and right concentration, belonging to the second zone, our mind training goes beyond restraint from harmful actions to actually trying to control the mind. *Mindfulness,* in this context, means being mindful of the nature of impermanence and aware that all contaminated things—including our body and our existence—naturally bring suffering.

Right concentration is more than mere freedom from gross distraction and dullness. This concentration can easily focus wherever we direct it, with clarity and stability. This is a fundamental base for the development of compassion and altruism (mental factors of the second zone) and the realization of emptiness (in the first zone).

This second-zone mind of calm abiding is defined as a mind that is totally free from subtle dullness. Even when we learn to focus our minds, we may still experience laxity and dullness, which means that we have not yet attained calm abiding. Calm abiding has great clarity and intensity.

When more fully developed, these mental factors will lead to the development of the mental states of the first zone—nonattachment, nonhatred, and nonignorance. The first zone corresponds to the last two aspects of the noble eightfold path, right view and right thought. Right view is understanding reality, which from a Buddhist perspective is emptiness. Right thought is the other facet of the path, compassion and love.

COMPASSION AND SELF-CONFIDENCE

Loving-kindness, altruism, and compassion are important in the second zone because the corresponding second-zone *unwholesome* mental factor, self-centeredness or self-concern, is one of our primary mental afflictions. The self-centered, selfish mind is driven by and created from ignorance of the relationship of the law of cause and effect. The best antidotes to this mentality, which assumes that our own welfare is always more important than that of others, are the minds of loving-kindness, altruism, and compassion.

We need to distinguish here between the self-centered mind and the self-confident mind. Buddhism asserts that the self-centered mind is a wrong mind, but this has nothing to do with having self-confidence. Without confidence in our actions, such as our practice, we will be unable to achieve what we want to achieve, whether this be simple peace or full enlightenment.

In the same way, when traditional Buddhist texts state that the source of all suffering and problems is self-centeredness, they are not advocating self-neglect. The Buddha says in his first discourse, "The two extremes should be abandoned." One of those extremes is self-neglect.

Without addressing our own issues, it is impossible to understand what is going on for anyone else. The Buddha says, "Whoever loves himself will never harm others." Those who know exactly what causes pain or happiness for themselves—not intellectually but from the heart—will understand that it is the same with others. Love for both self and others is a deep love, requiring great wisdom and insight. In Sanskrit the word for this kind of love is *maitri*; in Pali it is *metta*.

Positive Mental Factors in the Third Zone

To achieve enlightenment we need the direct realization of emptiness and bodhichitta, and to realize these we need compassion, lovingkindness, and concentration. These might be too subtle for us right now, but there are mental states that we are quite capable of developing. These are the mental factors of the third zone. The ones I have included in the chart on page 82 are: mindfulness, calmness, equanimity, friendliness, joy, confidence, and optimism, as well as a correct understanding of cause and effect. Of course, this is not exhaustive, and I'm sure you can add many more positive qualities to the list.

Some of the positive qualities of mind in the third zone are associated with our emotions—such as friendliness or optimism—and others are associated with cognition—such as equanimity or mindfulness. One side develops our emotional health, the other side helps us fully comprehend the working of the mind, improve its positive qualities, and reduce the aspects that bring unhappiness.

Friendliness is not just showing a smiling face to others no matter what we feel; it means developing a warm, friendly character deep within, in relation to ourselves as well as others. Friendliness is an effective way of dealing with very gross problems such as loneliness or fear of loss. It creates strong connections with the society we live in and provides emotional sustenance for ourselves and the people we come into contact with. If loving-kindness is the simple wish for others to be happy, friendliness is the attitude we show toward others triggered by this most precious mind. Social isolation is a big problem these days. I read an article by a Western psychologist explaining why the problems of depression and loneliness are increasing in the West. Of all the factors he discussed, the one that made the greatest impression on me was the lack of belonging that many now feel. In the past, individuals belonged to a particular church, which brought a sense of community. Sadly, in current times this feeling of community is rapidly diminishing. Social interaction is very important in preventing loneliness and making us feel interconnected with our world, and friendliness helps break down the walls of isolation.

A calm mind is also crucial. Think about how our mind chases objects now, how we so easily become obsessed with things, exaggerating their qualities. Obsession is the opposite of calmness—it is a mental state of agitation. When clinging and obsession are present, we lose our mental balance. Calmness combined with mindfulness gives rise to the bud that will bloom into the flower of calm abiding.

I find optimism very useful in dealing with gross mental problems such as low self-esteem. Of course, all of our lives have negative aspects, but this is always only a partial picture. If we look into our situation honestly, we will see much to be optimistic about. For instance, we all have a unique and wonderful opportunity to develop ourselves. Understanding this great potential will naturally lift us out of feelings depression or low self-esteem. We can see that, even among people we have met personally, many beings have great minds—great wisdom and great compassion. These people are human beings like us and have developed their qualities using bodies similar to our own. The techniques they have used may be the same as those we are studying here. Like this, we can remind ourselves that the negative aspects of our existence are only a small part of our lives. Keeping things in perspective and recalling all the positive aspects of our lives, a great sense of optimism will grow.

Mindfulness, another important mental factor in the third zone, helps us both develop our meditation and deal with gross delusions. Resentment, anger, and vengefulness can never thrive if we practice mindfulness. Merely being mindful of what we are thinking acts as a mirror and give us the space to examine what is going on inside.

Mindfulness is also an antidote to the mind that obsesses about the past and future. Of course we need to prepare for the future, and memories are very important, but it is a kind of sickness to constantly dwell on what has happened before or what might happen next. Past memories and future daydreams can pollute our minds by preventing us from attending wisely to what is right before us. Present-moment awareness can also calm our minds as a preparation for meditation.

When I am feeling a bit low, I sometimes think about how everything is changing all the time, and it really raises my spirits. I can see that if I put effort into whatever is troubling me, it will make a difference. Things will change, regardless, because everything is impermanent, but I can recognize in addition that I have the ability to make it change in the way best for me. This kind of mindfulness I find very uplifting.

Work Toward Long-term Goals

Our goal is genuine compassion, so while we are making effort to develop these minds of the third zone and rid ourselves of our immediate problems, we need to keep our long-term goals in our mind. Keeping our motivation high and broadly aimed eliminates the possibility that we will become caught up in the seemingly trivial actions we all must perform each day.

Developing true compassion takes a long time. It will happen only if we remind ourselves continually that although at the moment we are working at developing positive qualities—mindfulness, calmness, a good character, friendliness—our long-term aim is the attainment of bodhichitta.

From the very beginning it is important to have a strong long-term motivation and to see that the positive attitudes we are developing now are part of a much bigger plan. There is no solution that can solve *all* our problems immediately—even the different aspects of the mind we are now developing will take time to arise together as the causes for bodhichitta.

Mindfulness shows us the picture—what is happening in our activities or our thoughts—but neither mindfulness nor the other third-zone positive mindstates are the main antidotes to the deep-seated unwholesome mental factors such as attachment, anger, and jealousy. Whether they are manifest in our mindstreams at present or only there in potential, these positive mindstates are the tools to develop the more profound positive minds of loving-kindness and altruism.

6 Epistemology: Conception and Perception

Epistemology in Buddhism

BUDDHIST EPISTEMOLOGY is the systematic investigation of the nature of knowledge: its scope, base, and reliability. It looks at the *scope* in terms of how far knowledge can go toward understanding reality, the *base* minds from which knowledge can grow, and whether knowledge can serve as a *reliable* source for an individual to completely understand reality.

Buddhist epistemology was first taught systematically and explicitly by the Indian scholar Dignaga (ca. 450 A.D.), and then by his commentator Dharmakirti (ca. 625 A.D.) in the *Commentary on Valid Perception (Pramanavarttika)*. As I have mentioned, although Nagarjuna and his disciple Aryadeva wrote texts on epistemology much earlier, this was not done in any structured or extensive way; thus Dignaga and Dharmakirti are considered the founders of Buddhist epistemology and logic.

Epistemology in Buddhism is not merely the study of knowledge for its own sake, but is aimed at bringing the seeker an understanding of how sentient beings can overcome their problems and eventually experience liberation—the cessation of suffering and its root causes. Dignaga and Dharmakirti's explanations of epistemology are not just empirical data, such as one would find in science—although of course much within their explanations concurs with Western science. The difference between them is the motivation. In the case of Buddhist epistemology, this knowledge is acquired solely to develop the understanding that counteracts and eliminates our fundamental confusion.

Conception

Buddhist thought recognizes two basic kinds of mental experience: the experience in which the mind accesses its object directly, and the experience in which the mind relies on another mind to access its object.

These two states roughly correspond to *perception* and *conception*, terms most speakers of English would understand, although not always precisely, and certainly not in the context of the Buddhist analysis. If you feel that a concept is a thought and a perception is more direct, more correct, then you are getting there, but even so, as we will see, there's a great deal more to it than that.

Dharmakirti defines *conceptual cognition* as "that consciousness that apprehends the object indicated by words in relation to the actual thing." Here we see a close connection drawn between thought on one hand and language and concepts on the other. In the definition, "words" refers to both language and concepts. In Tibetan the term for "word" is *dadun*, literally the "object of concept." That is not to say that a concept is the same as a word. An intermediary mind helps the mind as a whole access its object, and that can take the form of an image or an idea, as well as an actual word or label.

For example, think about a particular table, perhaps the one in your living room. When you think about the table, the image of the table will probably arise in your mind. That image can never be more than a representation of the table. A thought about the table is not the actual table. Between your consciousness and the actual table you are thinking about is the intermediary image of the table you have evoked.

However, the concept of table is more than just the intermediary process that occurs between the mind and the actual object; it also encompasses what we *mean* when we say "table." Our subjective representation of a table is not directly connected to reality because it is constructed by language and concepts. Thus, a conceptual mind is fiction rather than reality—it is made up by our minds. The concept is a subjective representation of an object that relates the object to other objects in the same class and is understood by society to be a whole. It is not the direct expression of the object.

Let's break it down a bit. We all relate to the concept of *table*. It represents an object with properties shared with all kinds of things— wooden tables, iron tables, simple tables, ornate tables, coffee tables, dining room tables—that have specific parts—legs, top, and so on— and function as table. This is a mental concept. The concept does not arise from the side of the table itself, but is part of our linguistic construction of *table*.

In reality there is no actual table that shares all the properties of every other table. We assume a common "table-ness," but that essence is fiction. The representation of the table in the conceptual mind is separate from the real table, and furthermore this fictional entity, table, that we hold is superimposed over any "real" individual table we are investigating. Our experience of a table is predominantly a projection, an abstract generality.

That does not mean the table does not exist. The object we call "table" sitting in front of us at this moment does exist, but the "table" of our conceptual mind only exists as a generality, because it is a mere conceptual construct.

CONCEPTUAL THOUGHTS ENGAGE THROUGH ELIMINATION

In the common division of existent things, Buddhist philosophers distinguish two categories: impermanent and permanent (which are categorized from the side of the object) or affirmation and negation (which are categorized from the side of the subject—the mind apprehending the object).

Although the former division is more widely discussed, in some ways the latter is more important because, from a Buddhist perspective, we can never know an object without the involvement of mind, and thus without some degree of subjectivity. Therefore, this twofold division contains objects that can be known by affirmation and those that can be known by negation. I would like to look at these now.

The conceptual mind does not apprehend its object through a positive recognition but by eliminating all other objects that are not that particular object. Therefore, in Buddhist epistemology the conceptual consciousness is construed as negative in nature, as it arises from a process of elimination.

For example, if I say "apple" to you, the image of an apple will come into your mind. According to Buddhist thought, it arises through the systematic negation of all things that are *non-apple*. If I qualify my concept by saying "green apple," your mind will refine the generic image, and my saying "That large green apple you have just eaten" will further refine it. Still, there is no direct perception of that just-eaten apple. The concept remains an elimination of all the stored memories of what is *not* that apple and a generic construct of what *is* that apple.

This process occurs through the use of a linguistic sign—a word or label. This is more than just seeing an apple and sticking on the mental label, "apple." The process is much more subtle than that. It is virtually impossible for ordinary people such as ourselves to have a direct perception of an object, unadorned by conceptual process. Even if we have no conscious discursive thought about the object, we engage in this mental process of object classification.

The negation process of conception has parallels in the way Buddhist practice is pursued. For example, this page is impermanent, but our minds presently perceive it as permanent, at least on a moment-by-moment basis. We need to eliminate the misconception that it is permanent to perceive it accurately. In this case, the concept of permanence is the object of negation. That is similar to the way the conceptual mind operates, though in this case we need to consciously intend the negation. Without negating its permanence we will never see its impermanence—either as a concept or, at a very advanced stage of meditation, as a direct perception.

We are categorizing things all the time. We classify objects as beautiful, ugly, tall, short, and so on. Moreover, our categories depend on our cultural context—so in one culture "beautiful" might be equated with tall, slim, blond, and blue-eyed, while in another it might be fat and bald!

We are also constantly making value judgments—good or bad, fair or unfair, right or wrong. Observing our personal instinctive dialogue of judgment is a very interesting exercise because value judgments as categories are particularly removed from the object at hand and say more about the perceiver than they do about the object. By looking at them, we can learn a lot about our minds. According to Buddhist epistemology, we arrive at our judgments—which are concepts—by elimination. On the basis of all of our accumulated conditioning, we decide that something is good by eliminating all that is not good.

Conceptual Thoughts Are Always Mistaken

The conceptual mind apprehends its object through negation, therefore it is considered a mistaken mind. Although it is a construct based on a linguistic, generalizing process that has little to do with the actual object before us, this is not the way we see it. According to our view, the object of our conceptual consciousness is real and accurate. This is a mistake.

As long as the dichotomy persists between *apple* and *non-apple,* or whatever our conceptual mind is apprehending through this elimination process, there is no way to overcome this fundamental mistake. Thus conceptual consciousness can never reflect reality as accurately as a perceptual consciousness.

A conceptual thought is merely a fiction projected onto an object or event and depends on socially shared assumptions. A table does not think of itself as a table—it does not think that it is wooden and comes from Ikea, or that its function is to hold a computer. These are all assumptions we attach to the object. In fact, the term *table* is a conventionality that exists in the English-speaking world. It has no reality based in the actual object. The assumptions we layer on objects arise from the social process of language acquisition and the habit of labeling our sense stimuli in certain ways over and over again. We want to buy a table, we plan the purchase in our minds, and we feel the table we want to buy is a real table, while in fact "tableness" is a fiction created by the conceptual mind and nowhere to be found.

Our experience of objects as real and our acceptance of the terms commonly used for such objects as natural are the two key factors for the formation of the conceptual mind. Superimposed on the real table is this combination of memory and socially constructed generalization that ignores the fact that one object labeled *table* is entirely separate and different from another object labeled *table.* In reality all physical objects are unique, individual things. In the realm of reality, this concept of *table* does not exist within all things we call tables; we superimpose it upon the object.

Conceptual Thoughts Provide Cognitive Content

Mistaken though they are, conceptual consciousnesses are vital to our lives and well-being. They provide the elaboration necessary for us to make sense of the raw data of the direct sensory consciousnesses. Only a conceptual mind can categorize objects; only a conceptual mind can analyze and discriminate; only a conceptual mind can plan—in short, only a conceptual mind can "think." Because of that, conceptual thoughts are very useful.

On one level they are always mistaken, misrepresenting the real world. On another level they are vital for sentient existence. They help us to apprehend things and events not apparent to our sensory consciousnesses, either because of their subtle nature, because of their temporal location—meaning they happened in the past or are still to happen—or because of their physical location—meaning they occur too far from our sense consciousnesses for us to apprehend them. In such circumstances the conceptual mind is the only way we can connect with those things and events.

As discussed above, we must strive to realize objects such as subtle impermanence and selflessness if we are ever to experience the complete cessation of suffering and its origin. Dignaga and Dharmakirti assert that such knowledge can only arise through conceptions. At our stage of development we cannot directly perceive subtle impermanence, thus the conceptual mind is the only tool we have to connect us to this truth in any way. Therefore, it is important to keep conceptuality in perspective. While we must understand that concepts always contain an element of error and do not reflect reality accurately, thinking is nonetheless crucial to our spiritual development.

IMPLICATIVE AND NONIMPLICATIVE NEGATION

If you asked a Gelug master about nonimplicative negation, he or she might just say that it is the most important thing you can ever know. It is such a strange term, and yet it is so important! Without understanding nonimplicative negation, it is impossible to understand ultimate reality.

The difference between the two types of negation lies in whether the negation causes something else to be implied in its place. Hence we have the terms *implicative* and *nonimplicative*. If you go to university where there are two choices, full-time or part-time study, and you tell a friend that you are not studying full-time, this is a negative statement. However, through this negation you imply a positive statement—that you *are* studying part-time. Thus your statement is an implicative negation. If I tell you there is no honey in the kitchen, that too is a negative statement, but it does *not* imply anything positive, such as the fact that there *is* sugar, or coffee. This is a nonimplicative negation.

Gendun Drub defines nonimplicative negation as:

> ...That which is realized through an explicit elimination of
> an object of negation and does not suggest some other positive
> phenomenon in place of its object of negation.[23]

In other words, a nonimplicative negation eliminates whatever needs to be eliminated without implying that anything exists in its place. To state that I don't play football does not imply that I do play tennis.

This may sound a little silly to you, but nonimplicative negations become crucial when we seek to understand emptiness or selflessness. We are all trying to understand emptiness (at least I hope we are!). But what are things are empty of? When we realize that all phenomena are empty of inherent existence, do we simultaneously realize that they possess other qualities? The insight into emptiness brings no such implication. There is nothing beyond, not even something called "emptiness." It is the same with selflessness. The very word directs us to the absence of a self, but it does not imply that something else exists.

Meditating on emptiness is a long and profound process. The object we are trying to negate is quite crude early on, but slowly it becomes more and more subtle. If, at the end of our analysis, we are left with anything positive at all, the analysis has gone wrong. Our negation should be nonimplicative. When our mind realizes an object's ultimate nature, its absence of inherent existence, what it realizes is just a mere absence of inherent existence and absolutely nothing else. If, when inherent existence is negated, anything remains—even something profound, like a realization of dependent arising—that mind does not have a true understanding of emptiness.

How the Mind Generalizes

Conceptual consciousnesses are mistaken in that the mind takes something generic and assumes it is specific. Superimposed upon the perception of a book, for instance, is almost always the concept of *book*, which helps us interpret the object but denies us direct access to it. There are four types of generalizations the mind makes about objects:

1. collective generality
2. categorical generality
3. meaning generality
4. sound generality

Getting a clear picture of these four points can really help us see the process by which we superimpose and the mistakes this process can bring. The effect of these mental mistakes is huge. In fact, the ways we react socially and individually to our world are dominated by these first three generalities.

A *collective generality* is really another name for the *density of whole*, a topic that comes up in the next chapter. In this context, however, we are focusing on the way the mind elaborates on the original sense data. *Collective generality* refers to the assumptions we make about the completeness of an object. For example, when we watch the news on television, we only see the top part of the anchorperson's body, but we assume the existence of his or her waist and legs. This is a conception rather than a perception. Our experience tells us that a person has all these parts, so if we see one part, we assume the others will follow. This is something we rarely question, and in most cases experience does not contradict it. However, this mistaken mind can harm us— even on a mundane level. Once, I was helping to renovate Jamyang Buddhist Centre after the building was first purchased, and I stepped on some old linoleum in a deserted upper-story room. I had assumed there was solid floor beneath, but in fact the floorboards were rotten— a collective generality that could have seriously injured me.

A categorical generality is a generalization the mind makes based on the category an object fits into. This can be a useful conceptual short-hand, but it can also be very harmful, as when we judge an entire race of people based on a stereotype.

No two objects are identical. Even if they are the same shape, color, and so on, they are two different entities. If you have two glasses in front of you, they may *look* identical, but of course they are different glasses; they are composed of different atoms. However, it would be impossible for the mind to keep up if it had to newly label every object in the universe every time it encountered one, and so we categorize. I have used *glass* as an example, and I know that you have no trouble imagining one. If I ask a friend to buy me a carton of soymilk at the shop, I know she won't come back with dog food. Placing objects into manageable categories is an essential role of the conceptual consciousness.

The worrying side to this mental process is that by categorizing, we may deny the unique integrity of the object. We may pigeonhole, reduce to stereotypes, or at worst, judge a person based on our generalized assumption about a group. The prejudice—racial, sexual, or whatever—that is the cause of so much of the world's suffering is probably the most dangerous manifestation of this. People under the influence of prejudice need no deep philosophical understanding in order to hate. If people with a particular bias—against a race, religion, sex, or skin color—see someone in that category, they react based on the categorical generality they are making. It colors and distorts their perception.

A *meaning generality* is another term for the generic image the mind creates. We have already covered the way the conceptual mind functions through image and language. Here the focus is the mental image that arises in place of the perception. As we have seen, the conceptual mind creates the image through negation, systematically eliminating everything that is not its object. So if I ask you to imagine an apple, the image that arises in your mind is everything that is not non-apple. No matter how specific that image might seem, it is not the actual object—it is the meaning generality. Say we both met His Holiness the Dalai Lama in Dharamsala in 1995 and I remind you that he shook your hand—a singular and powerful experience you are not liable to forget. That image may be strong and vivid in your mind, but it is still a meaning generality, a counterfeit of the actual event. In fact, we don't even remember real events at all for the most part; we recall our previous meaning generalities.

Sound generality is much the same, but based on sound. Think of your favorite song. In your mind you may hear it playing, although in reality of course it is not. This is the conceptual mind producing a sound generality based on memories of listening to the sound. Again, for the most part this process is harmless, but because the mind is not apprehending the object exactly in accordance with reality, a fundamental mistake exists that can cause problems.

These generalities operate continually in our minds. They shape our opinions and color our entire world, and yet we are rarely aware of them as such. Although this topic is complex, we should seek to understand it, for the misunderstanding that skews our view of the world, no matter how subtle, causes mistakes that can lead to suffering.

Perception

As beings of the physical world, we are fortunate to not only possess the ability to make sense of our external environment, but also to possess the five sense faculties by which we can gather accurate information about it. According to Buddhist epistemology, although perception is not solely the realm of the sense consciousnesses—on certain occasions the mental consciousness can directly perceive sense data—nevertheless our sense perceptions are the main tools by which we gain impressions of the external world.

Perception can be defined as "a mental event that can apprehend its object positively, engaging the object as it is." This refers mainly to our five sense consciousnesses. I walk down a street and see a person on the other side, hear the traffic, smell the flowers in the park, and feel the cool breeze. I am also eating an ice cream cone. These mental events—seeing, hearing, tasting, and so on—engage the object—the person, the noise, and so on—directly and positively. At this level there is no elimination or indirect apprehension.

Of course, things do not remain so simple for more than an instant.

Immediately the mind begins to label things, and feelings and stories arise. The person is a friend, the traffic is loud, the breeze is cold, and so forth. This is the conceptual mind's process of enhancing the initial perceptions, but they are not in themselves perceptions.

Intuitively, when we see an object, hear a sound, or ascertain something with any of our other sense faculties, we assume that it exists exactly as we perceive it. But all Buddhist schools assert a discrepancy between the world as it actually exists and the world as we perceive it. There is even a school that denies the existence of the objects of the external world entirely.

Aspect

When we apprehend an object through direct perception, we assume we are ascertaining the actual object. We see a house and we think there is nothing between the actual house and our perception of it. But this is not so.

Among the schools of Buddhist thought, there is actually no clear agreement on what we actually see. In order to get an idea of the complexity of this issue, we need to examine the assertions of each of the four philosophical schools. For our purposes, we will limit our analysis to the first three schools, excluding the highest school, the Madhyamaka, as it really complicates the picture.

According to the Vaibhashika school, the least subtle of the four schools, our consciousness has direct and unmediated access to the object. However, the Vaibhashika also assert that we are unable to perceive an entire object with a single consciousness. If you think about it, this makes sense. We see an apple and think we are seeing the entire apple. In fact our eye consciousness has only taken in the color and shape of the part of the apple we can see, not its back or bottom, or the smell and taste that make up the complete object.

But apart from that, say the Vaibhashika scholars, a real apple exists, and that is exactly what our eye sees. For that reason we call the Vaibhashika a *realistic* school. This is not because they have an exclusive claim on the truth, but because they proclaim that things are real in the sense of having an intrinsic essence.

This assertion is strongly refuted by the other schools. First, say the others, this assumes a chronological impossibility, for according to the Vaibhashika, the existence of the apple and the apprehension of the apple would have to happen at the same time. This would eliminate the possibility of cause and effect, which by definition is sequential. If the apple and the apprehension of the apple were simultaneous, then the object could not be the cause for the mind that apprehends it, which, according to the other schools, is absurd.

The Sautrantika and Chittamatra schools introduce the concept of *aspect* (Tib. *nampa*) in their discussions of how objects are perceived. The aspect is the reflection of the object that becomes the direct perception. It is an intermediary between the object and the mind, and as such behaves in the same way as a conceptual consciousness. We see blue, but what is it that differentiates blue from yellow before the conceptual consciousness labels it? These schools say it is aspect. The aspect of blue is both caused by the "real" blue color of the object and its representation in the visual consciousness.

It is obvious that an object cannot physically be present within a consciousness. However, according to these schools, the object can cause an impact—a mark or a reflection—on the consciousness. This is like leaning on a freshly-painted wall. Your arm is not left on the wet paint, but the mark of your arm is. According to these schools, this is a necessary part of the process of perception—without it, there is no base for discrimination.

The difference in assertion between the Sautrantika and Chittamatra schools does not revolve around whether the sense consciousness needs an intermediary, but around the status of the external object. The Sautrantika school assumes the external object exists, and the Chittamatra school refutes this. According to the Chittamatra, the aspects of color or taste that arise within our consciousness do not come about as a result of an impression from a real external object, but rather are produced by our own latent internal tendencies, or imprints. There is no experience of an external object without taking into account the mind that experiences it. Object and subject are one entity in that the table and the mind experiencing *table* arise at the same time from the same source.

Although having very different ideas about the subject/object relationship, both schools assert that a perception cannot arise independently of the object it perceives. Therefore perceptual aspects have a direct one-to-one correspondence with the objects they represent. A perceptual consciousness will arise only if there is an actual object, and therefore it can be said to hold the object itself. And so an eye sense consciousness apprehending a blue color is said to hold the actual blue even though it is only aware of the *aspect* of blue rather the blue itself.

Furthermore, an aspect is not something separate from consciousness. It is both a representation of the object in a consciousness as well as the actual consciousness that sees the object. Because of this double nature, it is said that the aspect has the *appearance* of the external object but the *nature* of consciousness.

The concept of aspect is also of great importance for these schools in that it opens the inquiry into self-cognition (Tib. *rangrig*),[24] or how the mind can apprehend itself. In relation to self-cognition, scholars such as Dharmakirti and Dignaga speak of two types of aspect, objective and subjective.

Objective aspect focuses on the object—the color blue, for instance—whereas the subjective aspect focuses on the eye consciousness itself as it apprehends blue. In any perception, two things happen simultaneously: the object is reflected in the consciousness—the objective aspect—and the consciousness is aware that the process is happening—the subjective aspect.

Almost all of the schools besides Vaibhashika—Sautrantika, Chittamatra, and Svatantrika Madhyamaka—assert that subjective aspect is a valid mind and that it is synonymous with self-awareness or self-cognition. They consider its presence absolutely necessary to trigger future recollections of the object. Dharmakirti says that cognition is *self-luminous*, which means that at the same time that the eye perceives blue, it is aware—self-aware—that it is perceiving blue. The meaning of *self-luminosity* is similar to that of the English term *apperception*, which means the mind's awareness of itself. These three schools assert that the mechanism by which we hold an object from one moment to the next is self-cognition.

The subjective aspect of a mind cannot be a different entity from the mind itself. If it were, for example, one mind looking at a separate mind, we would find ourselves in an infinite regression—for a mind apprehending an object, there would need to be a second mind aware of that mind, but that second mind would require a third mind that was aware of that one, and a fourth, and so on, ad infinitum. The subjective aspect is the *same* mind but a *different* aspect. The subjective aspect of an eye consciousness *is* the eye consciousness. It is the mechanism within the eye consciousness that allows the mind to later recall it.

Comparing Perceptual and Conceptual Minds

At this stage it is worth reviewing the two main divisions of consciousness, perception and conception, and expanding upon them. The chart below details this.

perception	conception
engages in its object positively, by affirmation	engages in its object negatively, by elimination
engages in its object as it is (without exaggerating)	does not engage in the object as it is
engages in a real object	does not engage in a real object
is generally very accurate	is always mistaken
does not provide any integrative content	provides integrative content

A perception apprehends an object without any labels or stories. It is not mistaken, unless there is some short-term physical problem, such as when we squeeze our eyes shut and see two moons. In contrast, as we have seen, conceptual minds are always mistaken with regard to their object.

It is not the role of the perception to identify the object; it apprehends only raw data. The conceptual mind then immediately adds the content and discriminates one object from another: eliminating what it is not, and identifying what it is, labeling it, and categorizing it. This process can also quickly arrive at a judgment about the object: good or bad, beautiful or ugly, friend or enemy, and so on.

Basically, all phenomena are either impermanent or permanent— there is no other alternative. Impermanent things depend on causes and conditions to come into existence and make up most of the *things* of our world. Permanent things do not function, nor do they depend on causes and conditions. Permanent things include states such as emptiness or concepts such as time. They do exist, but are unchanging, which is not to say they are eternal—they are not—but while they exist, they are not subject to cause and effect.

Impermanent things are also called *positive* or *established*, referring to the way the mind apprehends them, whereas permanent things can be called *negative* or *eliminative*.

Perceptions apprehend impermanent things positively. The eye sees a book—an impermanent thing—or the ear hears a sound. Conceptions apprehend permanent things. We can see how time and maybe emptiness may be permanent, since they are somewhat abstract to us right now. But what about the mind that apprehends a beautiful sunset? Surely a sunset is an impermanent thing? The actual sunset is, but not so the image of the sunset that the conceptual mind apprehends. That image is permanent, because it cannot perform a function and does not change moment to moment while it exists.

The sense consciousnesses operate without interpreting their apprehended object. When the eye sees something, there is no elimination process. According to some Buddhist schools, between the object and the consciousness is the aspect, which has a direct one-to-one relationship with the object and hence is nonmistaken. The sense consciousness sees the object directly and positively. The conceptual consciousness in contrast apprehends its object indirectly, through mediation, and negatively, through elimination.

A mental event is passive or active depending on whether a process is involved. The perceptual mind involves no process and therefore engages passively with its object. The conceptual mind, on the other hand, always operates through an intermediary and therefore engages actively with its object. A conceptual construct arises between the object and the mind—whether this be the label, the feeling of attraction or aversion, or any of the other sorts of elaboration that go on—the internal dialogue of comparison, judgment, and identification.

The perceptual mind only collects the raw sense data; the conceptual mind does everything else. The perceptual mind is like the latent image on the film in a camera—light rays hitting sensitized film. The conceptual mind develops and prints the film (and complains because it is out of focus!).

Usually, in our everyday lives, perceptual and conceptual minds work together. Directly perceiving a red traffic light and not going any further in the process is dangerous. We need the conceptual mind to label *traffic light* and *red* and enter into an internal dialogue that causes our foot to hit the brake. As we have discussed, however, the conceptual mind adds more information than is necessary, exaggerating and even getting it plain wrong. In reality, our partner is *not* the most wonderful person in the world (or the least), and this new flat screen TV will *not* be the key to never-ending pleasure.

Normally we experience the world around us without questioning it. Sights appear, sounds happen—they all become part of our experience, filtered, sorted, judged, and either filed or discarded. Unconscious of the mechanics of our mental life, we mindlessly develop attractions and aversions, we remember and forget, under the sway of mental addictions and habits. If we are ever to gain any control over this circus within our heads, we need to understand conception's power, and the way consciousness creates the world we encounter. We need to liberate ourselves from servitude to the negative conceptions that now dominate us.

Valid Cognition

Pramana

When direct perception is not mistaken with regards to its object, it is called *valid cognition*. In Sanskrit the term is *pramana* (pra MAH na; Tib. *tsema*), a term used in both Buddhist and non-Buddhist epistemology. Non-Buddhist schools generally use this term to refer to two things: an instrument for gaining knowledge of an object and the knowledge itself.

For Buddhist schools, pramana refers to knowledge itself. It is a nondeceptive cognition. Dharmakirti and Dignaga assert that a consciousness is only valid and correct if it is nondeceptive, and if that is so, then that consciousness is pramana.

In his *Drop of Reasoning (Nyayabindu)* Dharmakirti further states that valid cognition is a prerequisite for the fulfillment of all human purposes.[25] All roads to enlightenment must cross the threshold of valid cognition, says Dharmakirti. There is no use looking for fulfillment and happiness in anything if it stems from a mistaken mind, because sooner or later suffering will result. Without pramana, we might seek chocolate ice cream but end up with chilis. Of course Dharmakirti is referring to much deeper levels of mistaken cognition than this, things like seeing others without the lens of self-interest and seeing phenomena without the distortion of self-existence.

On a common-sense level, we can all see the truth in this. Misfortunes sometimes seem to come "out of the blue," but generally, when we suffer, we can identify mistakes we have made somewhere along the way. We make physical mistakes, such as not watching where we are stepping, or verbal mistakes, such as speaking without considering another's feelings—but the mistakes that matter most are made with the mind. The much-quoted Buddhist teaching is that the root of all our problems is ignorance, and that ignorance is the fundamental mistaken mind. It is not a mind of spaced-out nothingness, or a mind that simply does not know, but an active mind of mis-knowing. Therefore, it is vital that we understand and develop valid minds while eliminating those that are mistaken.

A valid mind correctly differentiates between existent and nonexistent objects. It can see that the horns of a rabbit are nonexistent and that the table in front of us does in fact exist.

The Etymology of Pramana

This Sanskrit term *pramana* is a precise technical term. Though I have not studied Sanskrit formally, I will try briefly to explain the term. Sanskrit words can be divided into base terms and either suffixes or prefixes. Grammatically, the word *pramana* can be split into the words *prama*, the base term meaning "knowledge-event," and *ana*, the suffix, which in this case is the active agent meaning "to bring about." Although *pramana* is generally translated into English as *valid cognition*, the term encompasses a broader meaning. The Western concept *knowledge* implies something enduring. In Buddhism, in contrast, knowledge is not static but momentary, and this is reflected in the use of the active term *ana*.

In the monasteries, as a learning tool, we divide the word slightly differently, into the syllables *pra* and *mana*. *Pra* has many different meanings depending on the context: among them "excellent," "perfection," "first," and "newly." *Mana* means to measure, cognize, recognize, or apprehend. So *pramana* literally means to cognize perfectly, excellently, or newly. Different schools interpret this differently. Prasangika Madhyamaka scholars, for instance, read the *pra* to mean "main" or "prime." For when it is taken to mean "first" or "newly," then only the first moment of a mind can be valid, which is limiting. We will come back to this point below.

Nondeceptiveness

For a consciousness to be nondeceptive, the outcome must be consistent with the intention, meaning the object we are seeking must be determined correctly. Suppose we are looking for our friend John in a crowd. He is tall, bald, and wears glasses, and we think we see him in the distance. The consciousness has apprehended its object. When we move to the other side of the room, we see that the shape we took to be John is in fact another man. However, directly behind him is John. We sought John and found him, so there is agreement between the goal and the outcome—the practical effect is nondeceptive—but there has been a deception of the intention in that our actual object differed from the object we cognized.

A valid cognition can be either a direct perception or an inference. Inferential valid cognitions are discussed below. For either kind of consciousness to be a valid cognition, it needs to be nondeceptive in two ways: in terms of its practical effect (you want A and you get A) and in terms its capacity to capture the object accurately.

This means that cognition is more than just getting things right—it is getting things right *intentionally*. The eye consciousness looks at the table and mind apprehends it, and there is no incongruity between the intention and the practical effect. However, there is no valid cognition between the eye consciousness seeing Dave and the mind mistaking him for John, since the intention and the practical outcome are not in accord.

NOVELTY

If, as I mentioned above, one takes the first syllable of pramana to mean *new*, then a valid cognition must know its object newly. In fact Dharmakirti states that: "With respect to this, valid cognition is only that which first sees an uncommon object."[26]

This element of novelty is quite important. Although a mental event that repeats previous information can be beneficial and may reveal correct information, because it is a repetition of a previous consciousness and therefore gives no new information, technically it cannot be a valid cognition. If it adds nothing new to the cognitive process, it is, in terms of cognition, irrelevant.

For example, according to most Buddhist epistemology, memory is not a valid consciousness, because it is a mere conceptual repetition of previous knowledge. There is no direct exposure to an object or event to ensure its validity, and so no matter how clearly and correctly we remember something, it no longer exists except as a mental fabrication. A nondeceptive mind must apprehend the object freshly. Thus memory can never be nondeceptive.

Gendun Drub wrote many commentaries on Dharmakirti, and he is one who claims that the *pra* in pramana definitely means *new* and therefore if a cognition does not reveal new information, it is not a valid cognition.[27] This view is widely held, but it can lead to complications. Khedrup Je, one of Lama Tsongkhapa's two main disciples, disagreed with the widely held view, arguing that novelty was not in fact a prerequisite for validity. He defined valid cognition instead as "the cognition that is nondeceptive with respect to the object that it [the cognition] realizes by its own power."[28]

So what does *by its own power* mean? It means without the help of another consciousness. Some masters assert that this implies a new apprehension, because a second moment of apprehending an object depends on the first moment. This does not refer to the general way that any moment of consciousness always depends on the preceding one, but to the specific way in which subsequent cognitions of the same object become dulled, losing the power of that initial moment. Here, we are *not* speaking of the conceptual minds that come into being immediately after any perception, but the raw direct perception itself, in its second or subsequent moments.

Other masters say the second moment of *perception* is still valid, but differentiate it from the subsequent moments of *mental* apprehension, the *conceptions* about the object. For them the idea of "newly" excludes only conceptions and not subsequent perceptions. If your definition of valid cognition is a mind that apprehends an object "by its own power," then second moments and so on can therefore still be *novel* if that apprehension is free of other minds—free, specifically, of conceptual superimposition.

INFERENTIAL VALID COGNITIONS

Within Tibetan Buddhism, it is generally agreed that there are only two sources of valid cognitions: perception and inference. Other philosophies also cite testimony, such as the words of a realized master, as a source of valid cognitions, or analogies that point to the truth, but these are disclaimed by most Buddhist scholars, including Dharmakirti and Dignaga.

As we've already seen, perceptual valid cognitions are simply our sense consciousnesses perceiving an object directly and correctly. To understand how an inference can be correct takes further consideration. Inference is a concept, and by definition concepts are mistaken minds, so is there a contradiction? We need to look carefully at the difference in meaning—within Buddhist philosophy, at any rate—between *valid* and *mistaken*. Some minds can be both.

Besides the usual twofold division of existent things into impermanent and permanent, there is also a division of phenomena into obvious, hidden, and very hidden things. *Obvious* things are things that we ordinary people can recognize without depending on inference, such as the everyday objects available to our five senses. However, our sense perceptions cannot apprehend *hidden* objects. To cognize such objects, we need inference.

The usual and very clear example of this is inferring fire from smoke. This is the example that eight-year-old monks love debating! When visible to our eye consciousness, fire is an obvious object. But it can also be hidden when, for example, there is a forest fire in the distance. All we see is smoke, but based on this appearance we can infer the existence of fire. This mind is valid because the mind accords with the object, although there is no direct perception.

It is the same with things like subtle impermanence or even our birthdays. We have no direct perception of the day we were born, not even a memory of it. We must rely on our parents' honesty and birth certificates. Despite all that, we still seem convinced enough to celebrate! Many of the really important ideas in Buddhism are hidden phenomena—emptiness, enlightenment, reincarnation, and so on. To understand and to finally realize such things definitely depends on inference.

The third category, *very hidden objects*, takes this all one step further. We can be certain that we are the product of our mother and father, but have no idea why we have a certain personality or why were born in a particular place. Buddhism says these things are due to karma, and at its most subtle level karma is a very hidden object. Very hidden objects can only be seen directly by a buddha and are thus penetrated by neither inference nor the direct perception of non-enlightened beings.

Through inference we can understand that we were born on such and such a date, which is a valid inference, but because it is a conceptual mind and not a perceptual mind it is still mistaken in that it does not apprehend its object directly. A conceptual mind is *always* a mistaken mind, even if it is nondeceptive. Seeing smoke and inferring fire is correct, or valid, but the mind that infers *fire* is also mistaken because it is conceptual and does not therefore directly apprehend its object.

Perceptions cannot apprehend concepts. My eye consciousness can apprehend the table in front of me but not the table's emptiness. For this reason, the conceptual mind of inference is a vital part of spiritual development, where we naturally move from a shallow, intellectual understanding of the concept of something like emptiness to a deeper one, and then to a valid inferential cognition. Without this, we could never go on to realize emptiness directly, and enlightenment would be impossible.

The belief that because conceptual minds are mistaken they are therefore never valid is erroneous, for it leads to the verdict that realizing emptiness or enlightenment is impossible. Only through conceptual minds can we attain such states. In order to avoid the dangers of acceptance based on mere dogma, we must understand epistemology well and employ valid reasoning. To do that, we must examine perception—the phenomenon that bridges the conceptual mind and the external object.

Many masters make this fundamental point: if we trace all valid cognitions back to their origins, we arrive at perception. Eventually any valid cognition—perception or inference—must be validated by perception. Seeing smoke in the distance and apprehending that there is fire is mistaken in regards to its appearing object—we have no direct proof of fire—but valid because there *is* fire. But this inferential understanding is only possible through the valid perception of smoke. And we are only able to ascertain and accept this link between smoke and fire because we have previously perceived this causal relationship.

Perception and conception continually work hand in hand to bring us a complete picture of the world.

7 Moving Toward Knowledge

The Sevenfold Division

PART OF EPISTEMOLOGY is the knowledge of conceptions and perceptions, and of mistaken and valid minds, as we saw in the previous chapter. Another part is understanding the actual way we move from mistaken to correct minds and from conceptual to perceptual consciousnesses. In its examination of the validity of knowledge and the way we acquire it, the Gelug tradition commonly lists seven types of mind:

1. wrong consciousnesses
2. doubting consciousnesses
3. non-ascertaining consciousnesses
4. correctly assuming consciousnesses
5. subsequent cognizers
6. valid inferential cognizers
7. valid direct perceivers

WRONG CONSCIOUSNESSES

Wrong consciousnesses, whether conceptual or perceptual, are erroneous with regard to the main object. Although a direct sense perception can be a wrong consciousness, the error will generally be very superficial. The traditional illustration is seeing everything as yellow because of jaundice—although wearing sunglasses might be a more modern twist on this example. In contrast, wrong consciousnesses at the conceptual level, such as belief in a permanent self, can be quite deep.

Buddhist epistemology lists six sources of deception:

1. the object
2. the basis of perception
3. the situation
4. the immediate condition
5. karmic imprints
6. repeated familiarization

I'll deal with the first source of deception last. The second, the *basis of perception*, is deceptive when we mistakenly focus on an inappropriate object. Many minds and mental factors make up a mental event, and usually the mind moves to the most important but not always. Something can skew our appreciation of the object. For example, a loud sound can blind us to an oncoming car as we step off the curb.

The *situation* can also deceive us. For example, we may view a large male figure on a dark street as intrinsically threatening when no actual threat is present.

The *immediate condition* refers to the immediately preceding moments of mind that distort our appreciation of an event. An example is when intense anger leaves a residue that colors the following situation, causing us to see something we would ordinarily experience as pleasant or neutral as negative.

Karmic imprints trick us all the time. In fact, the propensities left on our mindstream from past actions have almost constantly programmed us to mistake things. The most important mistake relates to the suffering of change, where we cling to objects as intrinsically desirable only to set ourselves up for future suffering when they inevitably "fail" us. The fault lies not in the object, but in our perception of it.

Similarly, *repeated familiarization* distorts the picture, dulling perception and making mistaken attitudes seem normal and correct. We see this with political rhetoric, advertising campaigns, and dysfunctional families when violence and selfishness are portrayed as desirable. It is also true of our habitual projection of self-existence onto objects.

These points are interesting to explore and, I think, reasonably easy to understand. But let us return now to the first source of deception on our list, the object. As I mentioned earlier, the object itself can also deceive us. The other sources of deception can be seen as subjective—they are all mistakes the mind makes. How is it that the object can be at fault?

In fact, the fault does not come from the side of the object, but rather from the inability of the mind to take in certain aspects of the object. These aspects are known in Buddhist epistemology as the *four densities*:

1. the density of continuity
2. the density of function
3. the density of object
4. the density of whole

Density is the word that English-language scholars use, but I prefer the Tibetan term, *nyurwa* or "quick"—as in, the object or event is too "quick" for the mind to apprehend.

The *density of continuity* refers to the mistake we make when we see a sequence of events in relation to an object and mistakenly impute them as simultaneous or continuous. The confusion arises because there the space of time between the first event and the second is so small. The traditional example of this is of an arrow that is shot through a thick sheaf of paper. To the naked eye, it seems that the arrow has instantaneously created a hole through all the paper, but in fact it has gone through each sheet separately, one at a time.

We see another everyday example of this when we watch a film. Each second of a film is made of twenty-four separate frames, and each frame is a still picture. Because the frames are run through a projector very quickly, however, the movement in the picture seems to be continuous rather than composed of discrete stills.

The *density of function* looks at a set rather than a sequence as in the first density, but other than that it is quite similar. For example, walking up stairs seems like one single action to us, but, if we think about it, we can see that it involves a complicated set of motions.

The *density of object* refers to the way we see an object as a whole rather than as a collection of parts. A black-and-white photograph in a newspaper might look like one image of continuous tones, but if we examine it closely we will see it is nothing more than a collection of dots. Our mind makes connections that aren't actually present in the object itself.

The *density of whole* refers to objects that look uniform throughout although they are not. I see the front of something and presume the back and sides are identical. I bite into a delicious-looking apple only to find the inside is rotten. We are always making assumptions about wholes based on knowing only parts.

Recognizing that objects trick us all the time helps disengage us from appearances and look for deeper realities. Some people encountering television for the first time think that the characters and situations in soap operas are real. Of course we aren't like that (at least I hope not!), but we might well get so wrapped up in a good film that we forget we are watching actors in fictional situations. And rarely are we conscious that the images we are watching on the screen are a series of still images.

This does not mean that objects and situations are utter illusions or that they do not function. They do function. A newspaper photograph functions as such, and merely because we fail to see that it is composed of many dots does not mean there is no photo. There is, however, an element of illusion at work that relies on our mind to fill in the spaces.

The lesson here is that we should not grasp onto things unreflectively, or take the labels our mind gives them as fixed. The capacity to create a little distance in this way can help us break the patterns that cause us so much unhappiness. This gap is essential for understanding reality and for reducing emotional distress.

Lama Yeshe offers a simple yet effective meditation.

> You check, you watch, your own mind. If someone's giving you a hard time and your ego starts to hurt, instead of reacting, just take a look at what's going on. Think of how sound is simply coming out of that person's mouth, entering your ear, and causing you pain in the heart. If you think about it in the right way, it will make you laugh; you will see how ridiculous it is to get upset by something so insubstantial. Then your problem will disappear—poof! Just like that.[29]

Wrong consciousnesses are minds that process the information about their objects incorrectly. This might seem a pedantic point but it is important to realize that there is a difference in Buddhist epistemology between a wrong consciousness, such as we have been discussing, and a mistaken consciousness. The Tibetan term for wrong consciousness, *lokshe*, means "reversed consciousness," implying a complete inaccuracy, such as seeing a flower and thinking it's a horse.

Mistaken consciousness (Tib. *trulshe*) is much more subtle, referring, as we saw above, to the conceptual mind's inability to perceive an object directly. As I have said, the conceptual mind is always mistaken in this way, whether or not it is wrong.

DOUBTING CONSCIOUSNESSES

The second of the sevenfold division is *doubting consciousnesses*. This is a consciousness that is uncertain, wavering between one conclusion and its opposite. Everyday we are asked to make numerous choices, from products in the supermarket to decisions at work. If you are like me, most of those choices will be colored by indecision.

In Buddhist teachings, great doubt often arises in relation to the question of the inherent existence of things. We can listen to a teaching on emptiness and initially feel it is some esoteric concept that has nothing to do with our lives. That is doubt not tending toward the fact. If we hear more about it and start to feel that there is some possibility that things do not exist inherently, as the teachings are saying, that is doubt tending toward the fact. This is a powerful initial step in weakening the force of wrong view. It is the beginning of the process of moving toward correct understanding.

Even the suspicion that things and events may not be permanent is a thought diametrically opposed to our normal patterns and is in fact a very profound mind. As Aryadeva says in his *Four Hundred Verses* (*Chatushataka*): "Even through merely having doubts, cyclic existence is torn to shreds."

In the sequence that leads us from wrong consciousness to direct perception, doubt is one of the first types of mind we want to eliminate. However, early on, healthy doubts that tend toward the fact are in fact positive minds. For instance, to doubt that this is the only life we have and wonder if there is a next life might lead us to think about it, research it, and from the understanding we gain, produce a positive result.

The danger of doubt is the unsteady mind that does not examine closely and stays stuck in a wavering state, under the sway of whatever view was encountered most recently. If, while doubting the existence of future lives and not having examined the issue carefully, we attend a lecture by a charismatic speaker who asserts there is no life after death, we may get caught up in the presentation and immediately grant it credibility. In order to progress on the path, we need to move beyond this chronic indecision.

Non-Ascertaining Consciousnesses

Every day millions of sensory experiences appear to our consciousness. Say you walk from your home to a nearby park. When you return, you might be able to tell your partner about the noisy dog, the new display in the shop window, or the leaves turning brown in the autumn chill—but in fact you do not ascertain the vast majority of sensory input.

If we could analyze our minds over a twenty-four-hour period, most of what we experience would fall into this category. Of course we pay attention when we walk down a street—our survival depends on it— but the mind cannot possibly take in everything. The mind must filter input to make sense of the world, otherwise it would be like receiving every radio station in the world at once. The majority of our mental events are consciousnesses to which the object appears but is not ascertained, meaning the object has been apprehended by the consciousness without enough force to register.

Similarly, we may attend to an object, but it fails to register deeply. There is no certainty about the object. We attend a talk on Buddhism, but two days later cannot recall what was discussed because the teaching did not penetrate our minds sufficiently. That is another example of the mind that apprehends the object without ascertaining it.

CORRECTLY ASSUMING CONSCIOUSNESSES

The fourth consciousness is the last of what is called the *noncognizing consciousnesses,* in that they are conceptions and not perceptions and so do not actually "cognize" or know their objects. Correctly assuming consciousness is a consciousness that conceives the object in accordance with reality, but in a fallible manner.

While the vast majority of our consciousnesses fall into the category of non-ascertaining consciousnesses, the majority of the minds that *do* ascertain the object are correctly assuming consciousnesses. We ascertain the object but only through assumption. This mind can be positive, negative, or neutral, and it is a necessary step in developing the actual mind of direct perception.

A correctly assuming mind draws its conclusion based either on no reason at all or on a faulty reason. We have heard it, it seems right, and so we accept it without our own reasoning or experience playing a part. Even if we do investigate it in some way, we don't take this far enough. Investigation ceases before there is a full, clear understanding and whatever we are investigating becomes incontrovertible; it assumes without fully knowing. *Correctly assuming* means just that—the mind is correct about its object but it is only an assumption, without the weight of detailed analysis or realization. Very often cultural assumptions are taken as truths without investigation. I know many Tibetans who are very simple, devoted people who recite mantras every day and have unwavering faith in the law of cause and effect, but possess no understanding at all of subjects such as the four noble truths.

Because this consciousness assumes rather than knows, it has no

real power to actually recognize the object. We learn about impermanence and assume that things are impermanent, which is good to a
point, but the whole thing can become quite dangerous if we become
content with our limited analysis and never go deeper, especially if
our assumption is accompanied by a good deal of intellectual egoism.
Generally in Tibetan Buddhism we talk of three wisdoms: the wisdom
of hearing, contemplating, and meditating. Correctly assuming consciousness belongs to the first and is only really useful if it leads to the
second, which takes whatever it has understood to the next level and
eventually leads to single-pointed meditation upon the subject.

SUBSEQUENT COGNIZERS

The last three of the sevenfold division are cognizers, minds that actually get at the object. A *subsequent cognizer*, as the name implies, is a
cognition of something that has been apprehended previously. It is
subsequent to an initial and fresh valid cognition—either a perception
or an inference. It is not the first moment of that mind. My eye consciousness sees a pen. The first moment is a valid perception, the second moment is a subsequent cognizer. Subsequent cognizers can be
either perceptual or conceptual.

This distinction between *first* and *subsequent* is a point of debate
among Buddhist scholars—some saying subsequent minds are valid,
some saying they are not—but on a practical level, the difference is
not so important.

INFERENTIAL COGNIZERS

Although an inferential cognizer is a conception rather than a perception, it incontrovertibly realizes its object of cognition and, as such, is
as reliable a form of knowledge as a direct perceiver. However, while a

direct perceiver contacts its object directly and nonmistakenly, an inferential cognizer makes contact via inference with things that are not available to perception. Many points, such as subtle impermanence or selflessness, are at present obscured from our immediate experience and can only be comprehended through a conceptual cognition.

As we progress on the spiritual path, our capacity for logic develops and our understanding of hidden phenomena becomes deeper. Things that once were hidden to us and only accepted through the power of belief become objects of knowledge. Perhaps you have already had times when some level of understanding about a subject has come about, not through logical deduction alone but because some deeper comprehension has been triggered through a far subtler mechanism. You could call this intuition, but it could also be karmic imprints ripening due to meeting the right conditions. Buddhists call this a realization. You might have a good intellectual understanding of impermanence as a result of years of study, but all this knowledge can and should be solidified until it becomes incontrovertible. The mind that brings this about is an inferential cognizer.

Valid Direct Perceivers

Valid direct perceivers, the last of the sevenfold classification, are consciousnesses that apprehend the object directly and in a nonmistaken way. *Nonmistaken* means that no false element appears to the consciousness. The apprehension of the pen by the eye consciousness is without fault. What appears is the real pen. This obviously is a simpler concept of perception than the one we examined earlier, in which the *aspect* acts as a veil between mind and object.

The definition *nonmistaken* also eliminates mistaken minds that are not conceptual but also not direct perceivers. Sometimes certain sensory consciousnesses see or hear things completely incorrectly due to temporary distortions. While you are on a train that begins to pull away from the station, you may feel that the train is still while the people on the platform are moving. This is obviously mistaken. Although the perception of the moving people is a direct perceiver, it is not a *valid* direct perceiver because it is not nonmistaken.

In Buddhist epistemology there are four types of valid direct perceivers:

1. sense direct perceivers
2. mental direct perceivers
3. self-knowing direct perceivers
4. yogic direct perceivers

Sense direct perceivers operate with our five sense consciousnesses. *Mental direct perceivers*, on the other hand, are direct perceivers that are not part of the sensory consciousnesses. *Self-knowing direct perceivers* are also known as self-cognizers, the aspect of the mind that is self-aware and the source of memory. These minds are accepted as existent by all schools except Prasangika Madhyamaka, the highest subschool. It is worthwhile to look briefly at mental direct perceivers, which are said to be of two types: (1) those that occur at the end of a sensory direct perception and (2) clairvoyance.

Between the sense consciousness perceiving an object and the conceptual consciousness that superimposes conceptual thought upon the object, a brief moment of mental direct perception occurs. This consciousness is so brief that we ordinary people cannot recognize it. That moment is a mental direct perceiver at the end of a sensory perception.

The second type of mental direct perceiver is clairvoyance. There are different types of clairvoyance, such as the clairvoyance that directly sees other beings' minds, or the clairvoyance that sees their past lives. This kind of direct perceiver is developed as a by-product of the profound meditation of calm abiding.

Whereas clairvoyance is almost a side-effect of meditation, the development of yogic direct perceivers is a major goal of meditative training. Although we have the capacity to effortlessly and directly perceive such things as forms and sounds with our eye or ear consciousnesses, we do not have that ability with regard to profound phenomena like subtle impermanence or selflessness.

Through meditation and logical reasoning we start to understand subjects on an increasingly deeper level, moving from doubt to assertion to absolute conviction. However, at the beginning all of this occurs only within the conceptual process. In relation to impermanence, for instance, we get a stronger and stronger feeling for the momentary changes that occur in all things. The Gelug school says that a yogic direct perceiver realizing impermanence or selflessness directly—a perception—can only be achieved through the valid inferential cognizer—a conceptual mind. But through repeated meditation, that conceptual mental image becomes more and more part of our mind until it transcends conceptuality and becomes a direct perception. This is a yogic direct perception—we have realized the object directly, not through our senses, but through our mental consciousness.

Unlike clairvoyance, which is an achievement not exclusive to Buddhist practitioners, yogic direct perceivers occur only in the continuum of superior beings.[30] Although it shares some features with our sensory direct perceivers, such as freedom from conceptuality and being nonmistaken, yogic direct perceivers only occur through training. For this training, we need a clear understanding of the complete process of mental cultivation. The goal of having a yogic direct perceiver that realizes impermanence or selflessness seems impossible without understanding the definite attainable steps that get us there.

We start with conceptual minds, beginning at the wrong consciousness that sees everything as permanent. Through reading and listening, our doubts become awarenesses. For example, we may, after listening to or reading some Buddhist teachings, start to doubt that compounded phenomena are permanent. This doubt settles into a conviction and becomes a correctly assuming consciousness. With deeper reflection over time, it eventually becomes an inferential cognizer.

How do we turn these conceptual minds into a yogic direct perceiver? We need to develop calm abiding and then special insight, first separately and then together. The union of the two is not a yogic direct perceiver itself, but the tool that will help us develop it. Once we have done so, we can increase our realizations not only of impermanence, but also of emptiness and bodhichitta.

Remember that I said that there is no intermediary between a direct perceiver and its object, as opposed to a conceptual mind that is separated from its object by an image. Using the union of calm abiding and special insight—a mind that is simultaneously deep in meditation and possesses a strong understanding of the object—we can move beyond a consciousness reliant on mental images. When we separate our mind from these images, we are left with a direct perception of the very subtle object. Having gone through this process and attained this realization, it will never degenerate; it will remain stable from lifetime to lifetime. This shows the extraordinary power of the mind of yogic direct perception, and should inspire us to persevere to develop it.

Differences in Process Between Wisdom and Method

Examining this sevenfold division helps us see the process we need to undergo in order to attain enlightenment—from wrong consciousness all the way to a direct perception of the way things really are. There is a difference, however, between the wisdom approach and the method approach.

As you know, when we work from the wisdom point of view we address facts, such as emptiness or impermanence. But when we develop the method side of our minds, such as great compassion and bodhichitta, what we engage with is harder to pin down. Many texts explain that our conceptual understanding of emptiness or impermanence can become direct perceptions while we are still unenlightened beings. On the other hand, we cannot have a direct perception of bodhichitta until we attain enlightenment.

The reason for this is the object. Every mind must have an object. The object of a mind developing a realization of emptiness is emptiness itself. The object of the mind developing a realization of bodhichitta is the suffering of all sentient beings and enlightenment. We can manage to directly see the emptiness of, say, our own body—it is difficult but not impossible. But until we have an omniscient mind, it is surely impossible to directly know the entire suffering of every single sentient being.

Within the Mahayana tradition, this is considered the point of difference between individual-liberation practitioners and practitioners of the bodhisattva vehicle. When you realize emptiness directly, you can go on to attain liberation from suffering, but if your goal is complete enlightenment or buddhahood, the focus of your meditation is the suffering of all sentient beings. Liberation can be achieved within lifetimes, it is said, but enlightenment takes three countless great eons.

According to our tradition, both perspectives, wisdom and method, need to be developed in tandem. In the first stages, both are conceptual minds, but we develop them in different ways. Then, it is comparatively easily to transform our wisdom into a direct perceiver, but the same is not true of method. Certainly, the objects of bodhichitta and great compassion can be realized before enlightenment, and we can have very powerful experiences in relation to them, but they cannot be realized *directly*. In the context of the sevenfold division, they do not become direct perceivers but only correctly assuming consciousnesses.

In the texts on *lamrim*, or the graduated path to enlightenment, the topics of calm abiding and special insight are taught after bodhichitta. In Tibetan Buddhism, and particularly in the Gelug presentation, we do not develop these later subjects in great detail in the early stages, focusing instead on laying the groundwork of study. However, my feeling is that without calm abiding and special insight we cannot experience direct realizations of anything. The earlier topics within the lamrim will remain intellectual exercises and not penetrate our consciousness in any deep way until we have engaged with them in stable and deep meditation.

The direct perception of emptiness starts at the path of seeing, the third of the five paths of a bodhisattva. This is a very subtle mind, and there is a risk, especially in the advanced stages of meditation, that we will be led into a blissful equanimity from which we will not want to emerge. It is said in some Mahayana sutras that when many individual-liberation practitioners get to a certain point, the wisdom realizing emptiness becomes a meditative absorption that can keep them in blissful stasis for many eons. Our goal is full enlightenment for the benefit of all beings, and if we keep this in mind then we will not get waylaid along the path.

It is difficult to develop this mind while we are still trying to deal with the gross mental afflictions that plague our daily lives. The layers of the mind must be systematically unpeeled to expose evermore subtle layers of affliction. Happiness—of ourselves and others—depends on reaching these deeper levels of mind and developing both wisdom and method in our practice. And in order to bring this about, we must cultivate a deep understanding of the mind and how it functions.

The understanding of the mind that is the subject of the Abhidharma and Pramana texts has been developed over centuries by masters who have been not only great logicians but also great meditators. Their theories have been formulated not in isolation but in the laboratories of their own minds; they actually experienced the mental states they write about.

I feel that so much of this understanding is not only relevant, but vital to our lives today. Our world is in crisis now, a crisis caused largely by an ignorance of the real path to happiness. Look about and see if this isn't so, in your own life, in the lives of the people you know, and in the way the cultures of the world are developing. More and more, the spiritual is being set aside for material pleasure; deep, lasting contentment for the quick buzz. This is due to an ignorance of the role the mind plays in creating happiness and suffering.

In our greed for possessions, we are eating the world we live in. Gandhi said that the world has enough for human need but not for human greed, and it is greed that we see manifesting so strongly in our lives today. Possibly there is no more greed today than in previous times, but with the increase in population and advances in technology, we now have the ability to destroy the delicate infrastructure of this planet. Wisdom has always been needed, but never more so than at this moment.

We have all the tools necessary for a great transformation, of ourselves and of the world we live in. All we need is an enquiring and persevering mind. Mind is complex, but not unknowable. The subjects covered in this book deal with understanding the mind and using that understanding to transform it. As with any tool, whether you use it is entirely up to you.

Appendix

The Fifty-one Mental Factors[31]

ALWAYS-PRESENT MENTAL FACTORS

(1) contact (2) discernment (3) feeling (4) intention (5) attention

OBJECT-ASCERTAINING MENTAL FACTORS

(6) aspiration (7) appreciation (8) recollection (9) concentration
(10) intelligence

VARIABLE MENTAL FACTORS

(11) sleep (12) regret (13) general examination (14) precise analysis

WHOLESOME MENTAL FACTORS

(15) faith (16) self-respect (17) consideration for others (18)
detachment (19) nonhatred (20) nonignorance (21) enthusiasm
(22) suppleness (23) conscientiousness (24) equanimity
(25) nonviolence

Main Mental Afflictions

(26) anger (27) attachment (28) self-importance (29) ignorance
(30) afflicted views [the view of the transitory composite; extreme
views; views of superiority; views that regard unsatisfactory moral
and spiritual disciplines as supreme; mistaken views]
(31) afflicted indecision

Derivative Mental Afflictions

afflictions derived from anger:
(32) wrath (33) vengeance (34) spite (35) envy (36) cruelty

afflictions derived from attachment:
(37) avarice (38) self-satisfaction (39) excitement

afflictions derived from ignorance:
(40) concealment (41) dullness (42) faithlessness (43) laziness
(44) forgetfulness (45) inattentiveness

afflictions derived from both attachment and ignorance:
(46) pretension (47) dishonesty

afflictions derived from all three:
(48) shamelessness (49) inconsideration for others (50) unconscientiousness (51) distraction

Notes

1   For more on this sutra, see volume 1 of this series. The Theravada tradition is the Buddhism preserved in Sri Lanka, Thailand, and Burma, whereas the Mahayana tradition encompasses the Buddhism of Tibet, China, Korea, and Japan.

2   The four seals are: all compositional phenomena are impermanent; all contaminated phenomena are by nature suffering; all phenomena are empty of self-existence; and nirvana is true peace.

3   Gyatso, Tenzin, the Fourteenth Dalai Lama, *MindScience: An East-West Dialogue*, ed. by Goleman and Thurman (Boston: Wisdom Publications, 1991), p. 16.

4   Yeshe, Lama Thubten, *Becoming Your Own Therapist* (Boston: Lama Yeshe Wisdom Archive, 2003), p. 89.

5   *Subtle matter* is physical but is not visible or measurable by instruments, and its existence is thus not corroborated by modern science. In this example, the eye sense organ is a subtle material organ that resides within the eye and mediates between the eye and the visual consciousness. Subtle matter also plays a role as a vehicle for the subtle consciousness, much as the gross physical body, including the nervous system, is a vehicle for the gross consciousnesses. It is the so-called subtle body that the mind rides upon during the intermediate state between rebirths.

6   Buddhism describes three realms where beings live—the desire, form, and formless realms. The latter two realms are attained through deep meditative practice and do not depend on gross physical bodies. The desire realm encompasses six kinds of rebirth: hell beings, hungry ghosts, animals, human beings, jealous gods, and gods. The goal of Buddhism is to escape the cycle where one takes birth after birth in the three realms through the force of contaminated karma.

7   Rabten, Geshe, *The Mind and Its Functions* (Le Mont-Pèlerin, Switzerland: Editions Rabten Choeling, 1978), p. 20.

8   Dzogchen literature uses the term *rigpa* somewhat differently. The Tibetan word for mind mentioned previously, *lo*, refers more to mental states rather than basic knowing. *Sem*, which corresponds to the Sanskrit *citta*, is another common Tibetan word for mind.

9   Gyatso, *MindScience*, p. 21.

10 *Dhammapada*, I:1–2. Quoted in Rabten, *The Mind and Its Functions*, p. 11.

11 Gyatso, *MindScience*, p. 16.

12 Yeshe, *Becoming Your Own Therapist*, p. 31.

13 *Isolate (ldog pa)* is a philosophical term for a mental abstraction of an object. Technically, it means the opposite of everything the object is not; e.g., the isolate of apple is not-not-apple. One and the same object may produce different isolates depending on which aspect is being considered. Chapter 6 explores this aspect of conception in more detail.

14 For an explanation, see Rabten, *The Mind and Its Functions*, pp. 142–51.

15 The twelve links are: ignorance, karma, consciousness, name and form, sense bases, contact, feeling, clinging, craving, existence, birth, and aging and death. For an explanation see Tsering, Geshe Tashi, *The Four Noble Truths* (Boston: Wisdom Publications, 2005), p. 93.

16 For a more traditional account, see Rabten, *The Mind and Its Functions*, pp. 137–62.

17 The terms *mental affliction, afflictive emotion, negative mental state*, and *negative emotion* are different translations of the same term (Skt. *klesha;* Tib. *nyönmong*), one that is hard to render fully in English. It encompasses all the unwholesome mental factors discussed in the preceding chapter and has both cognitive and affective dimensions. Their effect is a disturbance in the body and mind that obscures perception.

18 Shantideva, *A Guide to the Bodhisattva's Way of Life*, V:13, trans. Batchelor (Dharamsala, India: LTWA, 1981), p. 41.

19 Shantideva, *A Guide to the Bodhisattva's Way of Life*, VI:20, p. 63.

20 Shantideva, *A Guide to the Bodhisattva's Way of Life*, VI:10, p. 61.

21 Shantideva, *A Guide to the Bodhisattva's Way of Life*, VI:41, p. 67.

22 Rabten, *The Mind and Its Functions*, p. 135.

23 Cited in Dreyfus, Georges B.J., *Recognizing Reality: Dharmakirti's Philosphy and Its Tibetan Interpretation* (Albany, N.Y.: State University of New York Press, 1997), p. 244.

24 Of the four types of perception cited in these three schools—sense perception, mental perception, self-cognition, and yogic perception—the highest subschool, Prasangika Madhyamaka, denies the existence of self-cognition, saying that it is not needed for memory to function.

25 Cited in Dreyfus, *Recognizing Reality*, p. 288.

26 Cited in Dreyfus, *Recognizing Reality*, p. 304.

27 Cited in Dreyfus, *Recognizing Reality*, p. 303.

28 Ibid.

29 Yeshe, *Becoming Your Own Therapist*, p. 60.

30 A superior, or *arya*, being is one who has achieved the third of five Buddhist path levels, that of seeing. The five paths are: the path of accumulation, the path of preparation, the path of seeing, the path of meditation, and the path of no more learning. What is "seen" in the path of seeing is precisely this direct yogic perception of selflessness or emptiness. *See* Tsering, *The Four Noble Truths*, p. 139.

31 The renderings in this list are largely drawn from Geshe Rabten's *The Mind and Its Functions*, which is translated by Stephen Batchelor. See chapters 7–9 of that volume for short descriptions of each of these mental factors.

Glossary

ABHIDHARMA (Skt.): one of the three "baskets" of teachings from the sutras, relating to metaphysics and wisdom.

AGGREGATES, THE FIVE: the traditional Buddhist division of body and mind. The five are form, feeling, discrimination, compositional factors, and consciousness.

ARHAT (Skt.): a practitioner who has achieved the state of no more learning in the individual liberation vehicle.

ARYA (Skt.): a superior being, or one who has gained a direct realization of emptiness.

ASPECT (Tib. nampa): the part of the consciousness that acts as intermediary, allowing the perception to apprehend its object.

BODHICHITTA (Skt.): the mind that spontaneously wishes to attain enlightenment in order to benefit others; the fully open and dedicated heart.

BODHISATTVA (Skt.): someone whose spiritual practice is directed toward the achievement of enlightenment for the welfare of all beings; one who possesses the compassionate motivation of bodhichitta.

BODHISATTVAYANA (Skt.): the vehicle of the bodhisattva, or the bodhisattva's path.

BUDDHA, A (Skt.): a fully enlightened being: one who has removed all obscurations veiling the mind and developed all good qualities to perfection; the first of the Three Jewels of refuge.

BUDDHA, THE (Skt.): the historical Buddha.

BUDDHADHARMA (Skt.): the Buddha's teachings.

CALM ABIDING (Skt. *shamatha*, Tib. *shiné*): meditation for developing single-pointed concentration *(samadhi)*, the mind that is totally free from subtle agitation and subtle dullness.

CESSATION: the end of all suffering, usually references the third of the four noble truths—the truth of the cessation of suffering and its causes.

CHITTAMATRA (Skt.): the Mind-Only school; the third of the four Buddhist philosophical schools studied in Tibetan Buddhism.

CYCLIC EXISTENCE: *See* samsara.

DEPENDENT ARISING: origination in dependence on causes and conditions.

DESIRE REALM: the world system in which we live, said to be dominated by sensory experiences.

DHARMA (Skt.): literally "that which holds (one back from suffering)"; often refers to the Buddha's teachings, but more generally to anything that helps the practitioner attain liberation; the second of the Three Jewels of refuge.

DHARMAKAYA (Skt.): "truth body"; along with the rupakaya, one of the two bodies achieved when a being attains enlightenment; this is the result of the wisdom aspect of practice.

EPISTEMOLOGY: the study of how the mind acquires and validates knowledge.

FALSE VIEW OF THE TRANSITORY COLLECTION, THE: the ignorance that innately misapprehends the self as existing independently or inherently.

FORM REALM: the second of the three states of existence of sentient beings, said to be inhabited by beings of great concentration and with few sensory distractions.

FORMLESS REALM: the third of the three states of existence of sentient beings, said to be the peak of cyclic existence, a realm of pure mind.

FOUR NOBLE TRUTHS, THE: the first discourse of the Buddha; the four noble truths are the truth of suffering, the truth of the origin of suffering, the truth of the cessation of suffering, and the truth of the path leading to the cessation of suffering.

GELUG (Tib.): Tibetan Buddhist school founded by Lama Tsongkhapa, one of the four Tibetan Buddhist schools; the others are Sakya, Nyingma, and Kagyu.

GESHE (Tib.): the title of a teacher in the Gelug sect who has completed the most extensive monastic and philosophical training.

GOMPA (Tib.): prayer or meditation room in a monastery, literally the place *(pa)* for meditation *(gom)*.

HIGHEST YOGA TANTRA: (Skt. *anuttarayoga tantra*); the highest among the four classes of tantra; the others are action (Skt. *kriya*), performance (Skt. *charya*), and yoga tantra.

INDIVIDUAL LIBERATION PRACTITIONER: a practitioner on the path to liberation, as opposed to a universal vehicle practitioner, who is on the path to full enlightenment.

INHERENTLY EXISTENT: existing from its own side, without depending on causes and conditions or on a labeling conception.

INTERMEDIATE STATE (Tib. *bardo*): the state traversed by a sentient being between death and the next rebirth.

KARMA (Skt.): literally "action"; the natural law of cause and effect whereby positive actions produce happiness and negative actions produce suffering.

KARMIC IMPRINT (Tib. *bakchak*): the energy or propensity left by a mental act on the mindstream that remains until it either ripens into a result or is purified.

LAMA TSONGKHAPA (1357–1419): a preeminent Tibetan scholar and tantric master and the founder of the Gelug tradition.

LAMRIM (Tib.): the graduated path to enlightenment—the progressive presentation of the Buddha's teachings propounded by the Gelug school of Tibetan Buddhism.

LAMRIM CHENMO (Tib.): *The Great Stages of the Path;* the extensive lamrim text written by Lama Tsongkhapa.

LORIG (Tib.): literally "awareness and knowledge"; the preliminary monastic course before studying Abhidharma and Pramana, the two main approaches to the mind.

MADHYAMAKA (Skt.): the middle way; the highest of four Indian philosophical schools taught in Tibetan monasteries.

MAHAYANA (Skt.): literally the Great Vehicle; representing one of the two main divisions of Buddhist thought; Mahayana is practiced in Tibet, Mongolia, China, Vietnam, Korea, and Japan; the emphasis of Mahayana thought is on bodhichitta, on the wisdom that realizes emptiness, and on enlightenment.

NIRMANAKAYA (Skt.): emanation body; one of the two aspects of the form body *(rupakaya)* of a buddha, the one that can be seen by ordinary beings.

NIRVANA (Skt.): liberation; a state of freedom from all delusions and karma, and from uncontrolled rebirth within cyclic existence *(samsara).*

NOBLE EIGHTFOLD PATH, THE: the discourse of the Buddha in which he explains the various attributes we need to develop to attain freedom from suffering; they are: right speech, right action, right livelihood, right effort, right mindfulness, right concentration, right view, and right thought.

PALI: the ancient Indian language used in the earlier (Theravada) Buddhist canonical texts.

POISONS, THE THREE: common name for the three root delusions of ignorance, attraction, and aversion.

PRAJNAPARAMITA (Skt.): the perfection *(paramita)* of wisdom *(prajna);* body of Mahayana sutras explicitly teaching emptiness, while implicitly teaching the paths of the bodhisattva. *The Heart Sutra* is one example.

PRAMANA (Skt.): valid knowledge; the study of how the mind can know something incontrovertibly.

PRASANGIKA MADHYAMAKA (Skt.): the Middle Way Consequence school; the higher of the two subdivisions of Madhyamaka school, as opposed to Svatantrika Madhyamaka.

REALMS, THE THREE: the three states of existence in which sentient beings abide: the desire realm (our world system), the form realm, and the formless realm.

RUPAKAYA (Skt.): form body; one of the two bodies a buddha gains upon attaining enlightenment (the other is the dharmakaya); the result of the method side of the path.

SAMBHOGAKAYA (Skt.): enjoyment body; one of the two aspects of the form body (*rupakaya*) of a buddha, which can be seen only by arya beings.

SAMSARA (Skt.): cyclic existence, the state of being constantly reborn due to delusions and karma.

SANSKRIT: the ancient Indian language used in Mahayana texts.

SAUTRANTIKA (Skt.): the "Sutra-System" school; the second of the four Buddhist philosophical schools studied in Tibetan Buddhism.

SEALS, THE FOUR: the basic Buddhist tenets, also called the *four views* or *four axioms*. They are (1) all compositional phenomena are impermanent, (2) all contaminated phenomena are, by nature, suffering, (3) all phenomena are empty of self-existence, and (4) nirvana is true peace.

SHAMATHA (Skt.). *See* calm abiding.

SHASTRA (Skt.): a classical Indian commentary on the teachings of the Buddha.

SUTRA (Skt.): an actual discourse of the Buddha.

SUTRA PITAKA (Skt.): one of the "three baskets" of Buddha's teachings; texts containing of his public discourses.

SUTRAYANA (Skt.): the vehicle of the Mahayana that takes the Buddhist sutras as their main textual source.

SVATANTRIKA MADHYAMAKA (Skt.): the Autonomy school, the first subschool of the Madhyamaka, the other being the Prasangika Madhyamaka.

TANTRA (Skt.): literally, "thread or continuity"; a text of esoteric Buddhist teachings; often refers to the practices themselves.

TANTRAYANA (Skt.): (also Mantrayana, Vajrayana) the vehicle of tantra.

THERAVADA (Skt.): One of the schools of early Buddhist thought; the emphasis of Theravada thought is on liberation, rather than enlightenment; the name more commonly used in Tibetan texts, *Hinayana* ("Lesser Vehicle"), carries an inaccurate connotation of inferiority.

TRIPITAKA (Skt.): the "three baskets" of the Buddha's teachings; the way in which the Buddhist canonical texts are divided: the Vinaya Pitaka (relating to behavior), the Sutra Pitaka (relating to concentration), and the Abhidharma Pitaka (relating to metaphysics).

TWELVE LINKS (OF DEPENDENT ORIGINATION), THE: the series of causes and effects that keeps us locked in cyclic existence. *See* note 15.

UNIVERSAL VEHICLE: *See* Mahayana.

VAJRAYANA (Skt.): (also Mantrayana, Tantrayana) the vehicle of tantra.

VAIBHASHIKA (Skt.): the Great Exposition school; the first of the four Buddhist philosophical schools studied in Tibetan Buddhism.

VALID COGNIZER: a mind that knows/apprehends its object correctly.

VINAYA PITAKA (Skt.): one of the "three baskets" of Buddha's teachings, its focus is ethical behavior, such as monastic and lay vows or the administration of monasteries.

Bibliography

Dreyfus, Georges B. J. *Recognizing Reality: Dharmakirti's Philosophy and Its Tibetan Interpretation*. Albany, N.Y.: State University of New York Press, 1997.

Gyatso, Tenzin, the Fourteenth Dalai Lama. *MindScience: An East-West Dialogue*. Ed. Daniel Goleman and Robert A. F. Thurman. Boston: Wisdom Publications, 1991.

Rabten, Geshe. *The Mind and Its Functions*. Trans. and ed. Stephen Batchelor. Le Mont-Pelerin, Switzerland: Editions Rabten Choeling, 1978; reprinted 1992.

Shantideva. *A Guide to the Bodhisattva's Way of Life*. Trans. Stephen Batchelor. Dharamsala, India: Library of Tibetan Works and Archives, 1981.

Tsering, Geshe Tashi. *The Four Noble Truths*. Boston: Wisdom Publications, 2005.

Yeshe, Lama Thubten. *Becoming Your Own Therapist*. Boston: Lama Yeshe Wisdom Archive, 2003.

INDEX

About the Authors

 GESHE TASHI TSERING escaped Tibet in 1959 with his family at the age of one and entered Sera Mey Monastic University in South India at thirteen, graduating sixteen years later as a Lharampa Geshe, the highest level. Requested by Lama Thubten Zopa Rinpoche, the spiritual director of the Foundation for the Preservation of the Mahayana Tradition (FPMT), to teach in the West, he became the resident teacher at Jamyang Buddhist Centre in London in 1994, where he developed *The Foundation of Buddhist Thought*, which has become one of the core courses in the FPMT's education program. He has taught the course in England and Europe since 1997.

 GORDON MCDOUGALL was director of Cham Tse Ling, the FPMT's Hong Kong center, for two years in the 1980s and worked for Jamyang Buddhist Centre in London from 2000–2006. He has taken an active part in the development and administration of the *The Foundation of Buddhist Thought*.

THE FOUNDATION OF BUDDHIST THOUGHT

The Foundation of Buddhist Thought is a two-year course in Buddhist studies, created by Geshe Tashi Tsering of Jamyang Buddhist Centre in London, that draws upon the depth of Tibetan Buddhist philosophy to exemplify a more realistic approach to living according to the principles of Buddhist thought. The course consists of the following six four-month modules:

> The Four Noble Truths
> Relative Truth, Ultimate Truth
> Buddhist Psychology
> The Awakening Mind
> Emptiness
> Tantra

A vital aspect of the course is Geshe Tashi's emphasis on the way these topics affect everyday life. A mixture of reading, listening, meditating, discussing, and writing ensures that each student will gain an understanding and mastery of these profound and important concepts.

To find out more about *The Foundation of Buddhist Thought*, please visit our website at buddhistthought.org. To find out more about FPMT study programs, please visit fpmt.org.

Also Available from
The Foundation of Buddhist Thought Series

"Geshi Tashi's insights can be enjoyed by a wide audience of both
specialists and newcomers to the Buddhist tradition."
THUBTEN JINPA, *principal translator for the Dalai Lama
and director of the Institute of Tibetan Classics*

THE FOUR NOBLE TRUTHS
The Foundation of Buddhist Thought, Volume 1

In this, the first volume of *The Foundation of Buddhist Thought*, Geshe Tashi provides a complete presentation the Buddha's seminal Four Noble Truths, an essential framework for understanding all of the other teachings of the Buddha.

RELATIVE TRUTH, ULTIMATE TRUTH
The Foundation of Buddhist Thought, Volume 2

This volume is an excellent source of support for anyone interested in cultivating
a more holistic and transformative understanding of the world around them and
ultimately of their own consciousness.

THE AWAKENING MIND
The Foundation of Buddhist Thought, Volume 4

Geshe Tashi Tsering guides students to a thorough understanding of two of the
most important methods for developing bodhichitta that have been passed down
by the great Indian and Tibetan masters over the centuries: the seven points of
cause and effect, and equalizing and exchanging the self with others.

EMPTINESS
The Foundation of Buddhist Thought, Volume 5

An incredibly welcoming presentation of the central philosophical teaching of
Mahayana Buddhism. Emptiness does not imply a nihilistic worldview, but rather
the idea that a permanent entity does not exist in any single phenomenon or
being.

TANTRA
The Foundation of Buddhist Thought, Volume 6

Anticipating the many questions Westerners have upon first encountering tantra's
colorful imagery and veiled language, *Tantra* uses straight talk to explain deities,
initiations, mandalas, and the body's subtle physiology of channels and chakras.

About Wisdom Publications

Wisdom Publications is the leading publisher of classic and contemporary Buddhist books and practical works on mindfulness. To learn more about us or to explore our other books, please visit our website at wisdompubs.org or contact us at the address below.

Wisdom Publications
199 Elm Street
Somerville, MA 02144 USA

We are a 501(c)(3) organization, and donations in support of our mission are tax deductible.

Wisdom Publications is affiliated with the Foundation for the Preservation of the Mahayana Tradition (FPMT).